NAMING THE MOOR

NAMING THE MOOR

Keith Howden

PENNILESS PRESS PUBLICATIONS
www.pennilesspress.co.uk

Published by
Penniless Press Publications

ISBN 978-1-913144-74-6

Envoi. There is little new in these pages. Most of these poems have been previously published, although there are a substantial number of small and quite a few larger revisions, re-shapes and corrections. I'd like to thank the following publishers for the work they have done and for the trust they have shown in me. *Peterloo* gave me my earliest chance: since then *Post-Romantic Empire (Rome), Redroom* and *Smokestack* have helped and supported me: and my later and considerable thanks must go to *Penniless Press* for the tolerance and encouragement I've received. To all of those who gave me the chance to display my ideas, my themes, my obsessions and my predilections, my sincere thanks

My thanks too, to ASMR for the cover photograph of Hameldon quarries, Barley Top and their surrounding landscape, the country of my heart.

Naming the Moor

LYRIC

NARRATIVE

LYRIC

Naming the Moor

1. Forebears

I wear them, ranting bastards,
my blood forebears, children
of unforgiving creeds,
acid within their moor: malign-

religioned as their weather,
abrasive as their hinterland's
hostility, liming to nurture
a bitter soil. Arthritic minds

raised chapels, rheum endowed
harmoniums groaning a Zion
complicit with their wound,
foetal within their landscape's pain

of names rotted to debris,
their walls' atavism, their intake's
compliant apostasy.
We wear implicit the impress

of maps transmitted through
long generations to compel
blood's shared imbroglio
with the lineaments of our fell.

No logic nominates the ground
or sanctifies the contour's stain.
To understand the wound
is not to heal the pain

2. Farms

I rant them, catechism,
those garble citadels of the moor,
names conjured in the prism
of a wry religion's grandeur.

Grime, Limers, Bullion:
Myrtle Earth, Rush Candle, Mean Hey:
Jericho, Noah, Zion,
Egypt: Slate Pits, Folly.

I name them, blackened bibles
of intake's apostasy,
assume their gibber syllables
in a rammel psalmody.

Ratten, Feist End, Gibbet:
Nouch, Lench, Gorple, Doal,
White Riding: Old Nick, Boggart:
Wormden, Bleakholt, Bone Hole.

I chant their dearth oblation,
the fossil babels of the fells,
seized in their weather's incantation,
germane within their vowels.

Nut Shaw, Delph Brink, Coppy:
Mary's Chair, Tolerance, Love Clough:
Horsehold, Whittle, White Kink, Cronkie,
Windy Gate, Rake Head, Nab Rough.

I tell their gabble rosary,
blab chapels of that plangent zeal,
intone their plainsong irony,
barren and evangelical.

Famine Ridge, Further, Windy Harbour,
Wreck Beds, Bleak House, Stone Crop:
Slack Myres, Wet Head: Hard Labour,
Needless, Poverty, Barley Top.

3. Saltways' Catechism

Who names the moor?
'I,' said the drover.
'In Bastard Clough, through Sod's Toll, at Hard Labour,
christen the salt's power.'

Who psalms the moor?
'I,' said the curlew.
'At Love Clough, on Tolerance, over Sweet and Mellow,
chant the salt lanes below.'

Who pays the moor?
'I,' said the drunkard.
'Through Swiggit, round Ale Corner, in Tosspot's Yard,
salt tickles the landlord.'

Who knows the moor?
'I,' said the pony.
'Up Skidders' Bank, on Whip Hill, down Stumble Valley,
lugging the salt's economy.'

Who clothes the moor?
'I,' said the grass.
'By Meadow Head, in Horsehold, under Goodshaws,
ripped by the salt's traverse.'

Who cheats the moor?
'I,' said the shrine.
'At Jesus Wept, at Mary's Chair, across Zion,
concealing salt's religion.'

Who shapes the moor?
  'I,' said the track.
'From Rake Head, over Slate Pits, at High Turnpike,
with salt wounding my back.'

Who sweeps the moor?
  'I,' said the rain.
'Down Foul Syke, down Deep Ditch, down Filthy Drain,
salt to salt the waters run.'

Who shrives the moor?
  'I,' said the whip.
'From Jericho, round Hades, up Hell's Rip,
speaking salt's ownership.'

Who rules the moor?
  'I,' said money.
'Without me, Famine Ridge, Bleak House, Poverty,
salt worthless, the shrines empty.'

4. Barley Top

Came to the ruined, dry-walled farm
in one of the barren folds of the hill,
its rafters raking the wind, its barn
vanished, but on the spanning lintel, still

crudely but deeply chiselled was the name
I'd sought, the legend, *Barley Top*. It crooned
of my grandfathers' boyhoods, wasted time,
life undernourished on infertile ground.

Even now, though rushes and bog-tufts spread
and vaulted walls and dragged aside the door,
a different, limier green betrayed
land lost by and recaptured by the moor.

I thought of those old builders, the sour land
desolate, unpropitious to their hope.
The name declared an optimism and
sheep they must have kept, but *Barley Top*

spoke languages of pathos, the frail nimbus
of stillborn dream, and *Barley Top* broken,
crumbling at the moor's relentlessness,
was every foundered hope for me then.

Wind trapped and blundering among the stone
took me to times that solitary, wry,
my grandfathers acknowledged as their own,
shoeless before the turning century.

5. Faugh's Delph

You are a learned woman?
I was never schooled. Some things
I have knowledge of. *The herbs?*
They have surprising powers.
And this, you told the Court,
was where you met him. Yes,
I told you, in Faugh's Delph.
Why there? I have no answer.
And what was his appearance?
He had no appearance. *What form*
did he take? What shape of
familiar did he adopt? Was it
as a cat, a dog or perhaps
even a goat? Was he tailed?
None of those. I have said
he was a presence, one that
I understood. *What name*

did he have or give? He had
no name. He has, as well you know,
a million names and they
are all the same. *And that
you believe?* That I believe.
I have no reason to lie.
His mere presence was in the form
of its own explanation.
An explanation of what?
His presence was the world
as it is the world, the world
continually and consistently
as we meet and endure it.
And that, you believe? I do.
I hold no evidence to tell me other.
You will be hanged. I will
be hanged. He told me so.

6. Naming Farm

My father's father's feral
apocrypha rolled his father's
mage annexation of the fell.
Sick sheep, the halt ram Topaz

barking in frost, the black mule
Benjamin staggering lame
from winter saltways. His oracle
voices roared millennium,

a benign weather's imminence,
while snow suckled the bacon blots
of his flock's abortions and bones
buckled in rain. The milk goats

drooped shrivel tits. Winter strangled
and wind boiled the grasses
where beltane bracken brindled.
A delivery of voices

pronounced that place's site,
which slab to lay, the solemn grain
of rafters: where communion light
should hole the walls, each stone

a mad *Hallelujah,* every slate
a cracked *Amen.* Deaf hearing learnt
the stars' clattering turn, blind sight
swung angels on his firmament

to garrison sunset, tied tongue
catechised clouds. Another
delivery of voices slung
anarchic bulletins to blather

that place's name. The maul
possessed his chisel and something
arcane within the lintel
compelled his ouija christening

of *Barley Top*. What wry
epistemologies or hopes
conjured that alphabet queerly
occult in his disease?

Lime failed his intake ventures.
Flocks rotted. Halt Topaz died
and the mad currency of voices
crashed on within his head

No logic nominates that ground
or sanctifies his contour's stain.
To understand the wound
is not to heal the pain.

7. Greenteeth

Greenteeth. They named their horror.
The witch fell's schism
bred him their moor's familiar,
its instinct ectoplasm.

Winter carcasses bared his tooth,
ghost wethers bleated his hymns.
Black birds chanted him. *Greenteeth*
spun inchoate in their names.

His holt was stinking water.
They met his boggart gloss
in methane alleys, his cadaver
loom in the amorphousness

of mist. Scared genets skittered
the echoes haunting gullies
where euphemism slithered
syllables of his alias.

The Irish carving canals
felt him shudder the spade's plunge,
wince at the pick. In candle tunnels
heard the shibboleth revenge

of dialect name their fear.
Semantic in sour soil, he hung
cognate in sounds, his spectre
colloidal in their mouthing.

Greenteeth. In gnostic chapels,
Rechabite roarings congealed
his darker doctrines. Taradiddles
maimed their psalms. Heresy cawed

in anthems. A coven drum
tumped Amen. Hallelujahs spat
carrion to gorge the phantom
hermetic in the pulpit.

8. Neighbours

They claimed the moor for neighbour, etched their farms
- *Rake Head, Windy Harbour* - in acid parishes
where vision led. Names gaunt with truth dissenting
the seasons' rituals, crude as wind ranting
its barren testaments. Faith's harbingers, they preached
labour's utilitarian religion.

Trespassed their neighbour's cloisters, sacked his shrines
- *Nut Shaw, Barley Top* - where they commanded
walls built to stem or swerve his sour recoil.
Syllables relevant as famine, each name
the thing it was, security against
the moor's revenges. They staked his land their own.

These were their lime evangelism's chapels
- *Stone Fold, Wet head* - faith's proper prisons,
sites christened by the land's austerity.
With pulpit vowels, hallelujah consonants
denied the moor's religion, raised their psalms
apostate in their neighbour's mysteries.

Bibles of picks and ploughs, they consecrated
- *Old Barn, New Barn* - names nodding at hunger.
From laagered missions, won among the infidel
intake some scattered gestures of conversion.
Nothing recanted. No miracle redeemed
indigenous atheism in the grass.

The bald moor holds them now. The leper stations
- *Cronkie, White Riding* - where vision foundered
stand sepulchres to that dead neighbourhood
gospelled in names. Nobody stayed. No labour
prospered to breach the moor's truth. Nothing appeased
a god dissolved in different sacraments.

9. First Electric Street Lighting

Working with Edison
taught him the trick. *He* said:
'Lord succour Thy invention.'
Garibaldi was dead.

Darwin kicked the bucket.
Grace abounded. Textiles fell.
*H*e said, 'Heaven shall radiate
from Perseverance Mill.'

Wagner snuffed it. *He* bottled
filaments of carbon,
specimen spiders and said
'God and Nature are one.'

Marx croaked. They dropped him
in Highgate. Gladstone
had his flies stitched and Hiram
Maxim perfected his gun.

He said, 'View favourably,
O Lord, Thy purblind son,'
believing electricity
was revealed religion.

Huxley burned his Bible.
He said, 'I will make night
and day indistinguishable
with ineffable light.'

Kipling versed. *He* said, 'I will
hymn light's great Creator.'
In Perseverance Mill
faith's humming generator

sparked. The Dreyfus affair
dragged on in France. *He* said,
'Light steady and regular
shall colonise the world

and man fulfil his destiny.'
Six filament coils
were his anthem. Hardy
planned *Tess of the D'Urbervilles*.

Gordon died in Khartoum.
There was gold in the Transvaal
and the dynamo's psalm
in Perseverance Mill.

He said, 'Darkness physical
and mental for ever destroyed'
from the steps of his mill
to the expectant crowd.

The Irish Question's rancour
loomed. *He* said, 'One further time
Thou hast made man master
of dark in his upward climb.'

Somewhere in France, Pasteur
killed bugs. 'Let there be light,'
intoned the Mayor.
Six bulbs brawled the night,

Simpletons on the fell,
at the throwing of that switch
in Perseverance Mill,
thought the valley bewitched.

At Branau-on-the-Inn,
shagging in the Custom House,
the wife said, 'If it's a son,
Adolf's the name I'll choose.'

'Man is perfectible,'
he said. 'Hallowed be Thy name
for this, Thy miracle.'
The Fire Engine came.

10. The Bell

'It was a beautiful bell. They said,
once the *Great Eastern's.* Its tone
was sweet and ship-like, best bell-metal.
Not only had it traversed the world,
but polished acres of its bevel
contained it, an intensified reflection
of some grander universe. Our grime canal
was in there as some Nile or Amazon,
some river of the mind, exotic
in its growths, burnished and fertile.
Such pastures I shall never see again,
the dream parishes of my heart's ache.'

'My name is Taylor. I was in General
Management. That strange day, the canal
lay jelly, stinking in some feral
equipoise. Then later, near the Chapel,
heading home, stunned by a seething sky,
I heard God. His voice spoke of the bell.
I heard entranced my Lord's pronouncement
of a world more righteous - His anthem,
His psalm, enthroned in the bell's symbol
of rectitude and order. I did not hear of fire until
the telephone clattered through my dream.

Arthur Leedham. I was cashier at the mill.
That bell was worth a mint and I was
thinking so when I saw the beginning smoke
stride the canal, heard unmistakeable
snarlings of fire. Machinery and stock
were going up, the skips and beams ablaze.
My mind savoured the bell. thinking it possible
there must be some reward for saving it.
But smoke battered my eyes, my eyebrows

singed with heat. And it was valuable
that bell. Even hammering windows
melting in fire, I dreamed of owning it.'

'*Chief Fireman Bannister*. I answered
my telephone's twang, heard of the mill
ablaze. Our engine's clanging carillon
roused the moor's wraiths. At the shed, phalanxed
flames roasted the sky. The roof came down.
Smoke's livid spectres danced the canal.
Another bell was clanging, clanging inside
the inferno's rage. Our jets phantomed steam
before they struck. Girder, loom and wheel
were fusing to a grotesque, tormented
statuary. Whatever rang that bell
rang it for me. It haunts my every dream.'

'*Arson or nothing.* Bankruptcy's threat
and ruin loomed. For a week, we steeped
waste cotton and bundled fents in oil,
hacked clear the paths and alleys for our flight
along the canal. *And try to save the bell.*
I needed moonshine's courage then, but scraped
the match to burn his mill. The floor dreamed
moonshine: drunk, we watched the tinder's lust
bite on stacked beams and skips until
the flame surrounded us. Then we spluttered
in smoke, crawled pissed through our holocaust,
to moonlight blistering the canal.'

11. Equation

I wear him narrow minded,
my father's father, exile
from Barley Top, whose toad
So be it, Lord, whose servile

Amen, I early learned
were fox propitiation
of his Omerta godhead
whose *Hallelujah* equation

meant Heaven's ambush wrath
averted. Never the squander
barkings of a laudation faith
but gold return for his vendetta

redeemer, one equally engrossed,
his mafia Jehovah,
by acquisition, cash and lust.
The moor's witch anathema

claimed him, stirred apostate,
congealing his litanies,
vital and unregenerate,
usurped the Hebrew pieties.

renting his pew. A religion
barren as stone, severe
as hunger fermented his bone.
Barley Top clawed his fervour.

Its Eden anthems hauled him
in the years he blasted stone,
still acolyte of its prism
altar, its bleak persuasion.

Now trucks in crippled phalanxes,
testudo at the ginny's head,
emblem the moor's spent industries,
correlative of the cracked

apocrypha of his faith.
Lost intake strangles the slope.
Wind wrangles the rafter teeth,
unbuilds the walls of *Barley Top.*

12. Whitsun.

Listen: rearing into hills,
the road hymns release
from prison terraces,
promising somewhere else.

It leans a Jacob's ladder
to scale the encroaching moor
where tankers, fonts sour
with acid, clatter under

the fell's scowl. Lorries altared
with quarrying's process rattle
the day's matins, haul
out of shadow, shuttle trade

to further highways.
A changed prospect assembles
another landscape's walls
and different geographies.

Listen: the whining vehicles
of choirs traffic epistles
under the moor's oracles,
promising somewhere else.

Bladdering Whitsun's banners,
infidel wind shudders
the flexible architectures
of Zion where the boxed gears

of hymns grind parables
contesting sceptical contours.
A sermon's engine stutters
the road to Christian bliss.

Prayers broker a faith
alien to the moorhead's
agnosticism. The summit breeds
maps for belief's untruth.

Riding the landscape's quarrel,
the road makes manifest
different distances. Christ
inhabits the wind's swell

of blustering banners where
the tankers' daily religion
corrodes. The land's skin
is scored with acid: the moor

is yearly burned: the fells
jut, daily quarried. The road's census
tells only its traffic's use,
promising nowhere else.

13. At Barley Top

Brash in the moor's economy,
their outpost's arcane scrape
scratches a stone. Its irony
mocks their labour. *Barley Top.*

I wear that cipher name,
my witch emblem of the fells
where wind charnels a scheme
of supine stone. The lintel's

menhir mumbles the chisel's
runing, a wryness that honed
my father's father's parables
of hope dissolved in acid ground.

Now bog-cotton and rushes burn
its hearths, bracken panels the door,
lime's fossil taint runs stubborn
in intake garbled by the moor.

The name survives, its pathos
- faith's impotent contour
in the moor's relentlessness -
encodes their leper tenure.

Wind blundering the grass
conjures with bones. I mourn
my father's father, shoeless
under the century's turn.

14. Chrysanthemums

I chart a ribald pentecost
to map my father. I am
the child beside him, late in frost
allotments, the moon chromium

with cold, the path's steel tempered
to tuning fork, ringing my frisson
footsteps in tensile air. Then seized
on rigid rods, in iron

equipoise, I saw those planet
skulls of chrysanthemums, blight
icon worlds, iced element
of nowhere, their frozen orbit

stemmed higher than my breath
clouding in cold. Moon was
a brittle paleolith.
In that white starlessness,

snow spun a wafer spectrum
of crumbled glass. But nebular
and insensible, that system
burst its void paternoster

to sear my knowing. No faith
survived that existential kiss
of golem otherness, unbirth
of all pathetic fallacies.

Moon leered that orrery,
poising each automaton head
in nowhere's primal nullity.
Till then, no miracle released

the codes of emptiness whose curse,
green in my gut, spoke parable
of nothing's stoic universe,
of being's ishmael babel.

From then, we mortared chapels
in different stone. For him,
the moor's sour canticles,
scrape intake's whining psalm,

the hill's enigma prism,
wore God's undoubted signature.
Two crossed sticks' barbarism
nailed his profoundest rapture.

I map that frost damascus,
still coldly absolute,
my gethsemane dogmas
of the sprit's vacuum transit.

15. Apologia

I carve it with words' maul,
that mapping : *Barley Top* : redeem
the page's arcane lintel
with its ouija autism.

I map its prison landscapes,
its prisms of ancestry,
its esemplastic equipoise
in love's commodity.

Barley Top shapes my deity,
unfolds the castrate parables
of intake, the geld psalmody
in rank upland's syllables,

flares boggart and ineffable
in the mind's methane alleys, looms
amorphous in blood's garble
nothing. Its long anarchies

poise the apostate equation
congealed in ruin's metaphor
that spayed us the fell's children,
erotic eunuchs of the moor.

I map myself, bone puppet
of that taint blight whose stigma
revels in flesh's state,
ingrains the witch anathema,

eidetic and embedded in
the landscape's lie : articulate,
ferments in skin's palatinate
internecine, *Barley Top's* stain

usurping the litanies
renting my flesh. I know that mantis
whose numen is to fuse
nothing's barren enigmas.

I carve the icon index
occult within its avatars,
the infibulating paradox
hermetic in our altars.

A Language for Stones

i. Knarrez

Somewhyle with wormez he werrez and with wolves
als, Somewhyle with wodwos that woned in the knarrez.

This was a language for rough land.
Within its structures move the residues
of a more brutal world. An older rhetoric
asserts the echo rememberings
of a cruel supernatural.
Hard vowels trap the rituals of blows,
harsh consonants haunt with resonances
of the knapper's hand. Within its rhythms
exist the gestures of the primitive,
asserting fen and fell. Alliteration hauls
a syntax more of moor than meadow,
a grammar of rough transits outside the silk
civilities of assonance and rhyme.
The innate parables of its movement
acknowledge codes and hierarchies
of older and unforgiving gods
It makes a direct stab into the senses,
a word's sword leaving the page,
its onomatopoeic and alliterative assault
enclosing felt experience
in the first rituals of its making.
This language fights. Is a *knarre* sharper,
more threatening, harder than rock?
It carries an attachment to the thing
more energetic than aimless naming,
where sound and function are moulded,
propelled into the senses' world.
Faith moves in metaphors of rock:
such transits cannot exist in *knarrez.*

ii. Before

Before speech
were the harmonies
of constellations, the impulse
swinging the galaxy's spheres.

Before speech
were the oratorios
of magma, the sun's hymn,
the moon's choreography.

Before speech
were the continents' rhythms.
the sea's orchestration
of geology's anthems.

Before speech
was the music of stone,
the constrained instruments
of a symphonic underground.

Before speech
was stone's imprisonment
of earth's locked descants,
its psalms waiting release.

Before speech
were the mineral adjustments,
the counterpoint of ores,
the songs of the knapper's hand.

iii. A music for stones

Stone seeks its music. Manacled
in mortar, imprisoned in walls,
knows the direction of its longing:

remembering earth's orchestras,
the innate symphonies of land,
rings intuitive and stays

responsive to the hidden anthems
of its molten forming, to the psalm
continuity of its structures:

embodies the wet intricacies
and soft diameters of grass, the juice
hypotenuses of water's leach.

Within its caliper are the wind's hymns,
the latent animus and flex
of millennial seasons. Strike
and hear through geological time
the reverberations and assonances
of mildew's stellar mechanics,
of the seed's muscle, of the root's
slow hunger, rain's lisping appetite.

iv. Eolith

Am dawnstone:
earth-engined,
magma's muscle made.
Am millennia molten,
mystery moulded,
rock roost riven,
time tanged,
gorge gouged,
strata scar.

Am dawnstone:
man-machine.
knuckleduster knapped.
Am hand-hammer history,
percussion prised,
axe anthem,
skinscrape,
mind moulded,
flint flake.

Am dawnstone:
mother music,
sound strike sensual.
Am rhythm's ritual rousing,
seed surplus seeking,
dance-drum,
limbs lithe lift,
bounty beseech,
psalm sending

Am dawnstone:
enigma-egg,
dragonseed dropped.
Am conundrum carved,
genesis garden garbled,
axe anthem,
age acrostic,
time tangle,
puzzle pebble.

v. Runes

ab tells the moor's thigh,
black boulder muscled.
whose flex is seasons.

eb tells the vault's tears
whose fall from no face
speaks heaven's absence.

ib tells blood whose curdle
at the sun's bandage
grows the bones' wound.

ob tells the moor's eye
whose always staring
forbids the sun's escape.

ub tells flesh whose wound
by the sun's sickle
begets blood's boroughs.

bu tells the moor's thought
whose substance no substance,
whose icon is wind.

bo tells night's ball, earth's soul
whose silver scar in void
is skin's lost search.

bi tells day's ball, earth's rod
erect whose muscle plunge
and spurt bays increase.

be tells the bones' hydraulic
palace and prison
whose prism is pain.

ba tells the cipher name
whose wound and sound
unsayable fuels the stars.

1. Cracked Mary's Holiday

i.

That summer, the wrecked *Foudroyant*
whaled on the beach, her rig awry,
her terraces of cannon cant,
I feared, to blast my holiday

God out of his sky. That summer.
under a shrieking seagull,
Mama's heels pecked the wet bladder
of strand. There was the rank smell

of donkeys and hot sand. Papa's
boozed baritone hurled *What Are
the Wild Waves Saying?* at the sea's
equal intemperance. Later,

in a shell's telephone, I
begged to be loved. Another
seagull dropped shrieking, a donkey
hee-hawed. The sea said, none to spare.

ii.

That summer, I learned to fly,
rode the Big Wheel to value
a doll world under me.
Mama was the black sequin who

waved upwards, Papa the tipsy
tiddlywink. The greenhouse Winter
Gardens flashed sun. Epilepsy
twisted the world miniature.

Suspended, I learned flesh untoward.
Harsh kiss and impassioned hand
in the compartment corner ignored
a child. All they attained,

passion's squeals and grunts, I made mine.
I ached to be loved. The wheel
wound landscapes up and down.
Level gulls roared, not possible

iii.

That summer, the sham pavilions
on the pier's plank spewed flesh. So much
sweat and breath, like Resurrection's
pale millions blinking their retch

from earth, so much snot and skin,
a maggot's' dance, the mills' pupae
unearthed and wriggling in the sun.
Mama pouted headache. Papa

snored gin to his afternoon's
boredom. A few gulls shrieked for
gobbets. I posted sixpence
through boards to the sand under.

Eye to that slit, I watched them,
sprawled gropers in the pier's shadow.
I yearned for love but lust's drum
under me said, Not here, not now.

iv.

That summer, to the Tower's
 Longstone, I played Grace Darling,
at a polished sea pretended her water's
rodeo. An epsom salting

at the tide's crawl rim was my
lashed Farne. One gull's syllable
pumped my petrel and fulmar sky.
Mama I thought too stoical

at her rescue. Dear Papa
hiccupped at the benign swell,
tossed guts in a bored parabola
to that poised, hammering gull.

Papa bubbled vomit. A steamer
hooted. I craved love. A few
fish threshed in a box. Mama
said, Not for me, never for you.

v.

That summer, Mama said, No.
I, at Papa's insistence,
was hauled through new Meccano
lattices to the Tower's glans.

Sea had more weft than warp from there.
We gloated a diminished
and futile world together.
Then Papa jumped. I heard

his last hoot and saw him leave,
seagull spreadeagled in his last
drunkenness. He seemed to wave
goodbye. I had no tears. The rest

was newspapers' babel. They
dropped me between Meccano.
I dreamed of love. Reality
screaming the ground said, No.

2. Cracked Mary's Mill

i.

They call me mad. My father's,
his father's father's mill this was.
Now mine. Brick broken fingers
crude for the sky's soft pieces.
I watch through dolly-blue, false
curtain of my window-glass's stain,
cavorting children dance my walls.

Weeds reach to trip. I laugh in noon
green to the sun, stalk ruinous
my garden's tangle, my father's
paths, my mother's luminous
borders blown. Convolvulus
is snakes, still parasol cow-
parsley cracks. Elderberries
flutter my hand's rape. Now
among mossed Morrises,
dead Papa's cars, and fungus
Fords, Mama's, I twine green
by the burst walls' bellies.
Was once their mill. Now mine

ii.

Copperplate, indentured,
forty apprentice orphans
fevered within a week. Rye bread
so black and soft it clung the gums
like putty, sometimes porridge
sour and blue their foul diet.
Poor starvelings, before that rage
pestilence, death's appetite,
fell at their looms, committed
life on the cloth, were maimed by
senseless machines and screaming died.
Saw horrid visions. Secretly
at night, my father's father,
his father fired to clean the stall,
pitch and tobacco to deter
the fever's rampage, had girls sprinkle
vinegar to cure the beds

of retching children. So much death,
rumour swears their shallow sheds
unconsecrated heave beneath
Fords and mossed Morrises
of my tumultuous soil.
Some say their bones crack in these
blenched towers of weed, straddle
their flesh through elders, bulge in
fat palms of hut-high nettles
as another century's pain
whose squalor forces the rank grass.

iii.

I am the white flower's dance
in the night garden, twisting,
am moth and phosphorescence.
Am maiden silk trysting
with ghosts. Am seven veils bare.
My midnight garden riots
pregnant with phantoms. They are
here, those fevered unfortunates.
Fat worms have awled them. The gleam
belly of lodge butting the weir
quivers old anguish. I am
the cupped convolvulus flower.
In the stilled wheel's genital,
their screaming. My midnights breed
cold flames in the crumbled wall.
I am the white petal freed.
More than the mousing cats, these
shadows cluster. One of them
loves me. His name is Peerless.
Among mossed Morrises, in drum
landscapes we lie. He touches me

strangely. Oh, then the fine
champagnes of my body. Peerless
speaks secretly his passion.
I am my mill's Salome
at midnight nautches where,
damaged and exultant, I
dance the cracked flesh's grandeur.

Mapping the Moor
(for my father, 1904-1993)

i.

Maps draw their makers' minds,
chart the spirit's orreries to display
a different ghost. Under the land's
icon lies another geography.

My father's father's Lancashire,
my father's, mine records a sour
religion sucking austere
sustenance from the famine moor.

We knew a barren contour
of tight lips. Our maps sanction
no legend for the ardent or
lexicon for his death's occasion

ii.

On his old maps, curlews
named moorland over soot Maydays
in mill villages. Delirious,
arching to a remembered cause,

he shouted, *'Where's the accident?'*
No tracks invade that region
or charts presume that continent.
How do you tell a dying man

he is the accident? Precise
cartographies of the real
encode within their geographies
a shuddering spiritual.

On my new maps, Mercedes
commuters tart mill cottages
in the moor. Geographies
unchanged wear shifted images.

iii.

I mean our maps. A map dances
its maker's mind, sings somewhere
within its graphic assurances,
the spatial fables of another

and ineffable territory.
he said, *'I'm not much use at dying,
I've never done it before.'* In my
museum of charts, I hang

that ultimate cartography
of flesh's dependency, the bleak
boundaries of eternity
encompassed in a stale joke.

iv.

A blackened psalm-box heaving
harmonium bleaknesses
and hymnal caterwauling
into my moor wrangles its place

on all our maps. Within its cramp
marshalling yard, the menhir
regiments and the sooted pomp
of grocers' obelisks require

reveille's bugle where the fell's
bleak code and barren signature
ethic the self-denials
implicit in our contour.

And once, in sudden sunlight,
during alchemies of sleet,
I saw its prison railings bright
as a necklace of marcasite.

My father's father's Lancashire.
my father's, mine, records a sour
contagion mapping austere
apocrypha on our famine moor.

We sanctified a parable
of tight lips. Our maps' custom
denied a lexicon or scale
or language for love's idiom.

I mean a map. My map dances
its maker's mind, incarnate, rants
within its graphic assurances,
fables attempting sustenance.

v.

I mean a map. But how translate
the heart to flattened landscape?
This was a quarry grief and that
some outcrop pain. Can any map

encompass and hold retrievable
in paper correlatives,
the feint, uncopiable
lattices whose grid contrives

labyrinths in dimensions
that have no northings, eastings,
the transubstantiating zones
of the mind's rememberings?

I mean a map more than cartoon
similes and simulation.
But by what logarithm can
the heart's countries be known?

How make a chart so integral
that, subliminal, it maps
the making of itself, and all
shifting allegiances and shapes

lie esemplastic in its scheme?
I mean maps: lost parables
of barren farms, forgotten intake's
apocrypha, that sour religion's

anathema. I mean a map
whose arcane undertaking
is parthenogenesis, whose trope
the guile of its own making.

vi.

It is my map, but how to say
his dying moved me? Not the death
but the self's seismology
metamorphic within its myth.

My father's father's Lancashire,
my father's, mine, nurtured the sour
osmotic autisms that were
the instinct language of our moor.

We traded barren contours
of tight lips. Our maps deny
the ostentation of remorse,
the luxuries of threnody.

I scrawl a map above a map.
He said, *'I'm not much use at dying,
I've never done it before.'* This shape
I scheme on cellophane to bring

another map beneath and see,
by lineage or the chance
of duplicate geography,
an imposed equivalence.

'Why are they always,' she said,
such hostile landscapes?' She meant,
skirting the moor, the crowded
fables under us, the immanent

apostasies of the past.
I draw that map. The parables
of spent workings: the manifest
of ruins: the runes of broken walls.

And sometimes, jewelled sunlight
transmuting a thunder rain
has conjured dearth's palatinate
to the landscapes of Cockaigne.

vii.

On his old maps, curlews
named moorland over lost Maydays
in mill villages. Mine pursues
a shifting weather's ironies.

I make a map of time, one wry
and existential second stilled.
In it, on flat-cap holiday,
charabanc mashers are held

in equipoise, soot calyxes
of blossom seize in an opulent
embalming. Memory fixes
that howl of *'Where's the accident?'*

where simian, in oriental
attitudes of carved bone,
caged monkeys, for gawp's festival,
are staring tarsier from stone.

Fermata strangles the band's
tuba kazoo. Spring's anthem
of larks in the moor's hinterlands
is hushed. In sunlight's stratagem,

the swing-boat's stayed pelota,
straining at counterpoise,
preserves the stilled parabola
of its compliant prejudice

with death. Somebody's Woodbine
droops unlit. Somewhere a silent
palaver boils and someone
is shouting *'Where's the accident?*

A boat upturned farts sucker-cup
in the mill lodge's frame. Lost oars
skulk crocodile. On the bank slope,
a keyboard of drowned flesh infers

that bright day's gothic havoc.
Then larks rage unfrozen. The swing-boat
remembers its plunging arc.
The monkeys scratch their fleas. That shout

encodes its semiotic shriek
in a prism hiatus
where being resumes its antic
and clockwork nothingness.

On my new maps, Mercedes
commuters are tarting barns
in the mill villages. The past's screes
weather to capital's religions.

I chart an ironic anguish,
a map less to mean than be,
whose metaphor stalks language
for its implicit geology.

viii.

It is my map. Secret in my
chartroom's hangings, there is
that Chapel's long apostasy
carved in the soft integrities

of a living cell. Etched in
a dying mind's integument
is that Mayday mayhem: someone
is shouting, *'Where's the accident?'*

Deeply scrimshawed into bone
are landscapes of spent industries,
rank farms, the failing benison
of lime in intake's bitterness.

'Why, always for you,' she said,
'are they hostile landscapes?' She meant
the moor's immanence, the crowded
apocrypha of its taint.

The marshalled menhirs of a yard
necklaced in iron wait display.
Obelisk alleys are scored
intaglio on a dry eye.

We traded in a religion
of tight lips and knew no chart
for subtler exploration
of the geographies of the heart.

I mean a map whose contours
flex esemplastic, yoking
compacted doctrines to enforce
the textures of its own making.

I mean a map. My map stutters
its maker's mind, lisps somewhere
within its coded structures,
its apprehension of a queer

and more arcane peninsula.
He said, *'I'm not much use at dying.
I've never done it before.'* In a
museum of joke charts, I hang

that ineffable region
of flesh's state, the wry acrostic
of nowhere, dry-point within
my doubting dialectic.

Teamsheets

1. Dynamo

The wind is in the east and icy.
It is six months since Hitler died,
five since the explosion
that scoured Hiroshima and three
since Attlee ousted Churchill. Droning blurred
in grey November, a Lend-Lease Dakota,
wings bannering the red star's sign,
steers into Northolt's landing area.

Thirty-nine Russians dubiously descend
to the wet tarmac. Then, the taciturn
interpreter that the press soon christens
Alexandra the Silent. An east wind
is blowing. Not long ago, Stalin
condemned Prokofiev for the formal
intricacy of his style. *'Do Russians
need sheets?'* is the question at the hotel.

For fourteen thousand pounds, Chelsea
sign Tommy Lawton. Five-shilling tickets
tout for a fiver. The east wind's rain
soaks ration books in a bomb-scarred city.
A few journalists in grandstand seats
chatter dismissively, are unimpressed
by Russian training. Recently in
East Prussia, Solzhenitsyn was arrested.

Chelsea will sweep them off their feet.
Completely ordinary,' is the headline
in the Sunday Express. *'Don't expect poise*
from factory hands. Lawton will get
a hatful.' 'Chelsea will easily maintain
our football supremacy' avows
the People's columnist. *'These pale boys*
are far too slow.' An east wind still blows.

There is a collective gasp. The Russian
eleven shuffles from sweat suits and disports
the Dynamo colours. A dark blue strip
thrusts a pink D on breasts blustering in
a cold east wind. Their long blue shorts,
unusually, are bordered with white bands
and emerald green socks twist at the top
to white on these pale factory hands.

Worse seems to follow when each Russian
presents a large and colourful bouquet
to his opposite number. It has the scent
of dalliance, or worse, propitiation.
The crowd droops dumb at such unmanly
happenings, then gorges on chauvinist
gloatings and jeers. Only the sentient
see pennants flapping a cold wind from the east.

What happens is the unexpected:
inch-perfect passes from these hacks,
a new athleticism and such tactical
awareness, such spectacularly fluid
movement that leaves the English backs,
unused to such adroitness and precision,
looking bewildered. Stalin might well
condemn such intricate perfection.

Later, touring the blackened city,
they make their official visit to the grave
of Marx in Highgate and salute, though shopping's
still on the agenda. And eerily,
the rationed world feels less safe.
Sleet spits the tarmac where a plane,
a Dakota with red stars on its wings,
blurs out of Northolt. An east wind sets in.

2. Pauper Grave

Eleven in one hole:
the slab's team-sheet texture
hides in deep grass.
Among the solvent graves,
workmen are firing
the Corporation's leaves.
  George Musgrove,
  Dayman Derrick,
  Herry Dexter,
were here selected
for an away fixture.

Some scratch and losing team:
hard-fettled
professionals in the game
gave them no quarter.
Now smoke's applause
lifts from the leaves' smoulder.
  George Bridger,
  Wilfrid Widdowson,
  John Salkeld,
are holding on
to positions in midfield.

The names tell one
of the crap and beaten gangs
of second-raters:
the proletarian, grey
syllables rune defeat.
The score is history.
  Sam Thompson,
  Albert Atkins,
  Joshua Hemmings,
out of the match,
trundle on different wings.

Workmen who piss
the steaming leaves contend
the game's improved since then.
Jack Blades and Harold Knott
make up a rotten side
whose cup-luck brought
  disaster.
  Nothing here
  shows they found
supporters in
the crowd filling the ground.

Onkonkay

I remember either watching or playing a part in the Onkonkay game-ritual, which must have been between 1938 and 1944. I think it never occurred after that. We played it on the first of May as a male rivalry and pence-gathering to compete with the Maypoles of the girls. Fundamentally the rite, or whatever it might be called, consisted of someone dressed in an eared sack decorated by a few ribbons, restrained by as much rope as we could find and controlled by a figure with a pole. The beast, as we believed it to be, went through a series of performance antics – somersaults, leaps, rollings and stick-catching. We knew no history for such festival athletics. I know that we had no idea of what the Onkonkay really was or was intended to suggest. I imagined it to be some remembered monster or perhaps some mythical beast-man, some fearful relic of the past to be both celebrated and defeated. At the end of the game-ritual, the creature was brought to the ground and his protective sack pulled from him. This preceded the sharing-out of whatever pence had been collected.

The truth is sadly a distinct anti-climax to all this hope of any historic or fertility relevance. During the Great War of 1914-1918, the usually Central European keepers of dancing bears ceased to arrive. Smart youths, seeing the chance of reward, took over the role of the bear and copied the antics and commands of their keepers. Onkonkay was not, in fact the name of the imagined beast but was drawn from the song we sang about it, an imitation of the trumpet-calls of the bears' keepers to draw attention to their arrival For me, the Onkonkay remains a grand invention, a creature of the imagination. I might have wished things different.

Onkonkay

Choosing Onkonkay

Who born is torn?
Who fool this year's fool
stamps sacked in streets?
Who garlanded goes
gallivanting grasses?
Who ribboned rides
in chariots of children?
Who hurrah is coming?
Who torn is born?

Who torn is born?
Who fool this year's king
goes rutting ripe
his spawn among stones?
Who the beast battering
his balls' belief banters
his cod's concert, crowns
the groin's gallery?
Who hallows harrows?
Who torn is torn?

Who torn is torn?
Who king this year's king
hauls hallelujahs
horny on the heap?
Who the thorns' thane
is earl of elders'
ferment, fine fashioner
of haws' hieroglyphic.
Who harrows hallows?
Who born is torn?

Who torn is born?
Who king this year's fool
comes ribbons wrapped?
Who naked nerved, his guts
elastic, white as worms
has hauled out of him?
Who dies pelt peeled,
greengarbled, fool framed?
Who beware is coming?
Who born is born?

At the year's blasting

Onkonkay. Hurrah. At the year's blasting
his sacked annual, beware is coming.
Of the high heap his moorland pelt
drinks from black streams
under thunder feasts himself among
bright berries of Mountain Ash.

Spare on the black fell rules
the raped moor scours the waste tarns,
is thorns' lost king, the wind's beast
whose breath spring whose language stone
stalks the sour marches comes
trumpeting his sacked festival,

Moves now within his ponderous dance
comes yearly coiled in children
black strength yearly garlanded
in ribbons to drum trumpet his dance
among mean streets, carries fertility's anthems,
seeds' sureties. Hurrah. Is coming.

Manifesto

Am come.
Am bulgebear bludgeon born,
monster moormusting manumitted,
deed dirty dickdancing
ogle Onkonkay.
Am born.
Am come.

Am come.
Am cockcod coitus craving come,
filth flourish fleshfather found,
leglevering, liquorlusting,
outrod Onkonkay.
Am born.
Am come.

Am born.
Am Barabbas ballsbaron bred,
appleadder, adameve awake,
gethsemane griefgardening,
offence Onkonkay.
Am named.
Am born.

Am here.
Am grailgreen gallumphing grown,
juggernaut, jelly joy jumping,
gropegreedy, goatgroaning
obscene Onkonkay.
Am bred.
Am named.

Am bred.
Am rustrotten redeemer raised,
naturenaughty, knobknackered known,
prickprancing, pump promise,
outrage Onkonkay.
Am here.
Am bred.

Am named.
Am gnarled, nailnasty known,
claycorrupt, crackcraving come,
scapegrace sackcloth skinned
ogod Onkonkay.
Am ripe.
Am here.

Onkonkay shout

Am
anarchic
stinking sweet sack.
Onkonkay.
michief's mechanic.
Ay Addy Onkonkay,
madness make mine.

Am
kissing's
kind kingdom come.
Onkonkay,
licence's lust lord.
Ay Addy Onkonkay,
mating make mine.

Am
disorder's
daft dancing, dirty.
Onkonkay,
misrule's maker.
Ay Addy Onkonkay,
mischief make mine.

Am
grace's
goat godgarbled.
Onkonkay,
mademan, manmade.
Ay Addy Onkonkay,
mystery make mine.

Am
sacrifice's
sinful sack slain.
Onkonkay,
Sweet saviour,
Ay Addy Onkonkay,
mercy make mine.

Among Streets

Comes sack sacrifice
saluting somersaulting
rag-tag ribboned among
his bounding boys
comes father of fields,
our teeming Onkonkay.

Comes from fell furlongs
flesh flouting to affirm
blossom and berry
haul health and harvest
to hurt holdings
our teeming Onkonkay.

Comes marching militant
from the moor's mystery
among alleyways' aisles
shouts seeds' success
among leaping lads
our teeming Onkonkay

Comes strutting streets
tin-trumpeting touts
increase's enigma idiom
fertility's franchise
ballooning belly and bud
our teeming Onkonkay.

Comes limber lads larking
his pelted progress
marching May's magic
his prancing's pantomime
our sackcloth saviour,
our teeming Onkonkay.

Onkonkay flayed

O cruel boys short-trousered
spindleshanked have killed
my Onkonkay stripping his pelt
from a pale flesh. A king dies here lies now
an emptied sack beast dancing done,

bright ribbons' wounds untangled.
O cruel boys have stripped
burl hide to bare raw flesh beneath.
the naked twitching nerve,
the bleb sinew of this king's dance.

Peel his skin from him, his guts
elastic white as worms
they have hauled out. Each year
is born is torn ripped skin from flesh
this chrysalis king. Now counts and gloats
pence at the roadside. Is born,
is torn in Onkonkay's wreck.

O return to us king of elders' froth
lord of haws' ferment, crownclown
our street dance when blunt earth
ploughs from this time a year's space.

Landscapes with Handless Man

Gull

Slime paths we trod together. The river slices
through a steep turn, comes pumping a wet leather
over worn stone. Light's reflected order
shivered town's pulse. Over the water's thrust,
nightshift was clanging in new outcrop workings and
bulldozers ripped raw causeways in pale grasses,
fashioned bald ravage on the tortured land.

Jack jarred the gun to me. 'Young fool,' he said.
'This time or never.' I was unwilling
'Take it,' he said. I took it. We were quarrelling
over the river's shove. Then a trailing
squabble of gulls scraped over us. Tractors
were lumbering saurians coupling in mud,
lurching lamp-eyed in battered pastures.

Steam of thin mist was sweating laminate,
furring the river's throat. One gull swung wide,
rounding the water's arc. Puppet to all my crude
anger ununderstood against him, I
brought up his gun and shot. The hit bird folded
wings to itself. Mastodons in the outcrop dirt
blared barren challenges through the torn cold.

The shot bird plunged slack water, ripped the light,
set the whole river's banquet shuddering.
'Bloody young fool,' Jack said. The stuttering
tractors scored runes in a bald country,
searched starless frost with their headlights' flare.
'I've taught you better than that.' A long regret
was tearing me. He'd taught me better.

A latent anger lived in everything.
Jack wrenched his gun from me. The riddled bird
wrestled in faster water. Bulldozers reared
predators at the chancrous land and ravenous for
its violated flesh. His mate dropped to him,
hung with him, spun with him in the sucking
water-race hauling his white wreck downstream.

She twisted mist-skeins over his bump riding
down a pace stretch. In turbulent reaches
hovered at combing stones. Her mate's chase
bucked on the water's swell, swung sharply.
We lost him in foam countries, marked his stiff cruise
by her above, his eddying, sudden shifting
of ways with sticks through the mad shallows.

Tractors were famish dogs baying bald screes,
hunting the land in packs, pointing the spew
of anger riding between us. 'I'll never lend you
my gun again.' Jack's pain was spilling for
that penance bird. 'It's when I'm killed and gone
it comes with promises.' 'What promises?'
'Clear to you by the time you get the gun.'

Pit Accident

A bright day. Arthur said, 'Down on the floor
I saw his bloody hands.' Morning sun suckled
at chimney tits, drained a limp Guinness poster.
Bunched fists of cloud lay on the fell's counter.
'Two hands and nobody with them,' Arthur said.

Blown dandelions were spurting filament
parachutes, seeding the river's barren pasture.
A woman in a mustard-coloured coat
dragged her snot child through sun in the street.
'Whose hands?' I'd always known whose hands they were.

'No accident,' Arthur said. Pale sunshine knifed.
In the allotment an old man's stoop attends
a sprawled dog with a bleeding foot beside
a broken frame. 'Jack Denison,' Arthur said,
carving the sunshine's trivial accidents.

'I didn't stir a limb,' he said. A black cat preened
on the yard wall, cocking a dietrich leg
suspenderless behind her ear and showed
a patchy undergut. Pink nipples plumped
pregnant to her coarse tongue's assuage.

'Struggling in the dark.' Across the pen,
girls in bright dresses flickered the paling
to dancing dioramas. The globe sun
bubbled bright gold. 'All the time struggling in
the bloody dark.' Our Lady's spire pricked nothing.

Children were plunging gravel at wet mud.
'Something you don't forget.' Boys balanced upright
on spoke-starved bicycles, their thin arms folded
to a proud handlessness. Sharp starlings banged
from roof to roof. Some things you don't forget.

Landscape with Handless Man

It is my mind's country, that dog's-coat smell
of stagnant river scummed and pooled beneath
a sky domed and oppressive as a skull.
Kaleidoscope allotments are jaundiced with

the year's decay. Ripe elderberries blood
the bankside pens. Swifts at their gathering business
cleave the far fell. Grey, captive cloud
clings, wool to wire, on the fell's screes,

teases to thinness, tears away. Now thunder
mutters. Time-lapsed, a second lightning stroke
shivers the water's pulse. Our Lady's spire
pricks nothing where greenhouse windows shake

timpani to the thunder's bass. A sough
of shifting pressures swells in pregnant trees.
Loose felting slaps tattoos in alleys of
allotment huts. Wind moves in swaying marches

through the bankside grass, draws swallows on
the river's pooling crust. This is my heart's
landscape.   I know the eternal fashion
of bins and kennels in the stagnant yards,

thin runes of aerials in a grey sky-fall.
I know the red bus on the hill road and swifts
gathering degenerate. These are all
changeless. In clock-ring patterns, tethered goats

champ an unyielding twitch. In the playground,
swings creak unoiled where, among broken rods
of sunflowers, the middle-shift compound
their garden platitudes. It is my blood's

country. In buttress terraces that screw
the river's wrist, cheap runners on brass rails
swing the spent greens of curtains soughing to
a suck and pull wind's pressures at the sill's

slit ventilation. White and ignorant
of the blear, spittle spark of thunder sun,
Jack Denison lies handless, buffets at
his bedclothes like a netted penguin.

He tells his love's landscapes

Here swill my heart's landscapes.
Clock dandelions spit their filament
symphonies in the yards. Swifts cleave the hill.
Cloud on the counter fell
plunges. Loose feltings' timpani slaps
the long allotment's music. Wasps
forage and squander in the compost's rot.
Sharp starling regiments rout fallen fruit.

Here sprout my blood's boroughs.
Grass seed in barren constellations sows
the river's restless firmament. Stone
terraces plant my passion.
The red bus on the hanging hill-road furrows
my bones' infertile pasture. Black water mirrors
a bulb's pale onion. A smashed stool wallows.
The cinder yards spawn brawling sparrows.

Here blister my skin's passions.
Felled hay in hill-fields pastures her flesh's cry.
At the high lodgeside, disembowelled land
bares itself, arches its wound
of unhealed outcrop. The steep overflow shrines
cascading water. Under its bastions,
ravished, bemused, beneath its tower, we lay.
Swifts high and screaming pierce a bridal sky.

Here spits my seed's process.
Mountain ash spill blood along the fell.
Freed water thunders over the lodge's lip.
It was our Eden then, that deep
midgeridden gloom, that pooled sky, that rich sluice
bursting its business through a simple grass
in the deep hollow's wound, my green valley's fall.
The white boat bearing me is a murdered gull.

Here wasps my wound's legend.
Sunflowers' broken rods drip shrivelled grain.
She bred me spring and fall, my mallard pleasure,
my autumn's flesh, my year
with its fat bellyful. She swelled my knackered land
of goats tethered on twitch, my hands' playground
of summer's squealing swings, that barren garden.
Scrag bantams rut that parish's lost Eden.

Here stings my truth's ruin.
Chrysanthemum heads are frosted hard as moons
in the midnight allotment. There has been
falling and budding since. Once mine,
the clattering clockwork of arched heaven.
Was once a god. Once tore time's tawdry curtain.
Here rips my silly minute's fail and dance.
Bursting my planet, here come the filthy swans.

v. Landscape with Denison Dead

Mushrooms I had and I remember this:
my pockets ripe and spawning their musk milk,
that workless Monday with the sun's ballock
brawling in bits along the river mud.
Rain's early lumping polished the light. There was
a black cat sunstruck on a wall washed gold
and sunstruck, Our Lady's barren prick.
Sun pooled and jewelled in the allotment grass.

Under my hand, rich blackberries bulging
pulsed a juice blood. Jack was laid out upstairs,
a dead man lost and distanced under a spider's
labyrinth, missing the sunburst festival
flaring in spent allotments. The black cat's tongue
grew sudden sunlight and the criss-cross grill
of leaded glass squared the wax contours
of fallen face. Our Lady's spire pricked nothing.

Good beer I had, and when the pubs were closing
climbed to the fell where the land creases
and sours under the moor. Marching heat hazes
spun on the asphalt distances. The land raged dry.
Jack Denison, Arthur said. Pale sheep outcropping
were boulders on the slope. The spent drift lay
a rammel palace under us.
Denison's dead. Our Lady's spire pricked nothing.

vi. Landscape with Drift Mine

'Jack Denison,' he said. Afternoon's closing time.
We climbed into the fell where the land creases
and sours under the moor. Marching heat hazes
    spun on the asphalt distances.
    Pale sheep outcropping
stood boulders on the slope. Sun burned the calm.
Denison said the sunlight we were stepping.

Streams had burned dry. 'Jack Denison,' he said.
The worked-out drift lay sullen under us:
its iron guts bled rust into poor pastures.
    The fan ripped from its innards was
    a rammel palace now
for heat-dazed sheep. Roof and walls had decayed.
Denison said the torn fan's tumbled shadow.

We turned down to the drift. The moor waited.
The fell was bare and harsh in the sun's glare.
Town's petty straggle trailed the valley floor
    with stagnant yards, Our Lady's spire.
    Sheep didn't move
at our approach. 'Jack Denison,' he said.
Denison said the sun's long blare above.

'Jack Denison,' he said. His shoulder burst the lock
through its punk housing. I was afraid.
This was an eerie sepulchre of dead
    machines. Oil and thick grime encrusted
    blurred window panes.
Dust spurted through the stained sunlight we broke.
Denison said the stench of dead machines.

In the drift's dusk only that latent question
lived for us then. The blank machines were sullenly
hostile. In a grimed bench drawer, he
    reached for the torn Directory
    and shuddered from it
that unread message. 'Tell Jack Denison..'
Denison said the oil and thumb-stained note.

'Jack Denison,' he said. The note's insistence
sucked the room's air to a foul prisoning,
swelled in its mood of sun-trapped flies with something
    oppressive in their buzzing.
    The door seemed a release.
Outside clean sunshine streamed, heat garbled distance.
Denison said the boom of clustered flies.

'Jack Denison,' he said. In a charged air
the black flies fizzed, butting at dusty light
in the bleared windows. Then he tore the note,
    scraped it to secret in the grit.
    'I'm glad it's over.'
Either the buzzing ceased or ceased to matter.
Denison said the torn and shredded paper.

'Let him lie comfortable.' We went outside.
His hand swept over the spoiled valley floor
and far below Our Lady's pricking spire.
    White pigeons in a flicker
circled the sun. It was all sun. 'Jack Denison,' he said.
Denison said the moor and straggled town.

Pulpits

For the Rector of Stiffkey

Unfrocked for immorality in 1932: later evangelised from a barrel on Blackpool Promenade: killed by a lion while preaching from its cage in a funfair in Skegness.

i. To His Bishop, suggesting a truer Eucharist

Where mouths purse, your host is cash.
Your serpent rears to spit the oldest sin.
Mine makes a sacrament of flesh.
I damn the state's grocery of bread and wine.

My bread is dough of flesh to knead
in women's thighs. My wine is white.
My God, your bourgeois agape has unmade
God: my God, fervour and feast have quit

your celluloid ceremonies:
my God, you have table-mannered Christ.
But laying on of flesh outweighs
Baptism's mumble, the suburbs' Eucharist.

The subtlest mystery is flesh.
Metaphors don't transcend the physical
and mystics float concrete avenues. My splash
of truth incarnates the ineffable,

symbol and stuff of what we are.
I psalm the electric spasm,
Eden's blanc-mange, that blob metaphor
of immortality, the bones' ectoplasm.

I scorn your Altar's laundered, civil lie,
your Pulpit's social suavity.
My Eden anthems flesh. My apple
plumps for a subtler chalice's cavity.

ii. Letters from Blackpool

Queen of my heart, my barrel,
as you might guess, grows harder, but suits me
fitter than faith. There is much to do here:
you would enjoy it. Glass *Winter Gardens,*
as relevant to winter as my former
Ministry to truth, spawn girls, and a wheel
high as Ezekiel's now spinning on cash,
tows poor souls Heavenward but always,
like Mother Church, drops them to earth.
The plump, skirted fruit of the *Gardens*
swells ripe for horticulture and the *Tower's*
varicose thrust reminds me of something.....

Queen of my heart, my barrel
grows hard more often. Only my tongue
pierces the multitude. There is plenty
to see here: you would enjoy it. I play
between a fasting girl now spent and thin
as a Bishop's promise and a flea-circus
more instructive than religion.
Trams fixed and conceited as lawyers
pass the Public Lavatories where the sea wind
gropes among skirts. Fleas at their jumping
and the thin girl lying pale and exhausted
in the next booth remind me of something.....

Queen of my heart, my barrel
torments me. The sea beats heavily here:
you would enjoy it. It does not thrust
slowly tumescent into creeks but heaves
frustratedly in and out upon
a beach where girls splay thighs on donkeys.
Only faces here are flint. Women,
poor foolish souls, jostle to touch me,
hoping I might confer fertility.
This mad sea threshing its buttocks of waves
into breached groynes and thighs apart nudging
the pommel's plunge remind me of something....

iii. A Lion in Skegness

Now he hears his home sea. Only history
seems caged where the salt wastes of Lincolnshire
contend the sea's frontiers. Wind blusters,
a demagogue on the flats. All day the grass
shakes hand-grenades at the mud and panzer
cumulus manoeuvres the vault's corridors.
A storm sea roars habitual fascism.
This is a far cry from Stiffkey's Parsonage.
On its glittering estuary Boston's Stump
awaits the drone of Dorniers and Heinkels
in slow formation. Now, in pea-field and
long ploughland, Lincolnshire's Churches, steepled
magnificent as rockets, wait to obey
the Air-Marshal's ultimate command.

For a showman, not much of a pitch, but not
a cage. Skegness's windy sentry paddles
a spindle pier into the sombre levels
where time and sea running out deform
the losing light to a bleak propaganda
of coloured bulbs slung in a civil landscape.
It is a far cry from Stiffkey's Parsonage.
A newspaper with Spain for headline splutters
the bowling green's uneasy netherland
and recent rain has failed to wash away
the Blackshirts' lightning insignia striking
the seized garden clock. A sharp ear might detect
the radio's crackle and the dull drumbeat
of Europe on the horizon's other side.

More threatening and sinister than a cage,
these fun-fair girders in the declining light,
no place for a showman where the inmates
gape at the sideshows' glowing ovens and hear
the screaming clientele of mad machines.
Swastika spars and gantries of the rides
plume tracers in a darkening air. The dodgems
contend and crash not far from the staccato
snipers and oiled weaponry of the booths.
It is a far cry from Stiffkey's Parsonage.
The zebra light and shade provides sufficient
uniform for the dispossessed. Another
train-load will come, to fill their vacant places,
to lose their shoes and win bewilderment.

Now he hears his home sea and here history
provides a cage and a sawdust continent,
a lion and a man. A few stuka gulls
are shrieking outside. Some in the audience
sense the sandfly time's momentousness. Here comes
sortilege in a skin. Stiffkey presages
Europe's slow tumble in this lecherous
and tiny actor. And here at the end of it
is the body's cage broken as France, the chest's
cavities exploded as Dresden, the ribs
ripped to Coventries and a belly butchered
as Dachau. It seems a far cry from Stiffkey's
Parsonage, this breath's broken economy,
the poor clown filleted by a mad lion.

Phyllis Dixey in Burnley 1959

Rituals deny surprise. What to expect
is on display. The ivory stalactites
of legs descend a drift of fur uplifted,
just concealing the bits that bulging butchers
will grope with eyes, debauch behind cold counters,
palp and possess in dreamland's orgies, rattling
their predatory tills. Giaconda Eve
smiles her long knowledge of the likely event.

Her monochrome portrait teases where Burnley's
tulips are squirting erect in April drizzle.
One breast, smooth and circular as a dartboard
poises its bull and inner on a froth of fur.
Tomorrow, the gallery's randy Goerings,
weighing topside, will coax its nipple taut.
She stands, Marilyn luminous, where the skin's
fascists are raising flesh's Nazi salute.

Rituals rarely surprise. The storm-troopers
of fumble fantasies are rallying to
their Nuremburg of tits. Stranded, she
seems a lost liner among the sweating tugs
of stale sensuality. Coy concealments
of chiffon flutter her *Aphrodite's* loins.
Butchers are howling their myth of a magic
and incorporeal meat. She lives outside.

She stands now almost naked, vulnerable
before them, in the daft trappings of half undress
but stays unreachably a dick's dance outside
their grubbing dream. Front-row Himmlers
rave her ritual. Black stockings process the aisles
of her thighs. Her suspenders glint amulet.
The Norman arches of her belt are colonnades
enclosing an altar. She is Mary serene.

Now the lecheries of grocers assault
the peeling dog-ear of pink sticking-plaster
legalising her crotch. On the mind's screen, she stands
dew-limbed as Venus on her shell. Gross lust
batters her tableau's bogus gentility
but something in the sumptuous flesh escapes
the air's bacterial and miasmic taint.
She seems innocent within innuendo.

Rituals mock surprise. She is different.
Something elusive populates the space
her thighs' parting allows. The ridiculous
is banished. She is now the sacrosanct truth
of slits and mounds. Even in prurient frills.
she sustains her myth. A cool morality
breathes her crevices. The Goebbels balcony
howls catcall propaganda. She eludes them.

Her breasts are sacraments, her nipples devout
as catechisms that the crap soldiery
of seats will never mumble. She is Mary,
Marilyn. Comes on the mind's screen, in Burnley,
in the drab fifties, this Eve before knowledge.
And not long afterwards, the insidious
religion of cancer groped her, invaded her,
tumbled her with the lust of a butcher's dream.

Warpaths

1.

Air Men

This is that golden England. Always in black and white.
These are its mythic villages, their never streets always
striped zebra in an always sun, high summer's ever habitat.
And they await you here: the irascible but finally all-right
blimp Colonel, the Rector smirking his rose-garden praise,
the garrulous postman, old maids with boudicca bicycles
whose heron profiles hide a softened heart. And always, the threat

that lived in wartime cinemas where dust and V-sign fingers
garbled the moonshine's passage to the screen. There too,
stood the Control Tower, alert, ceaselessly sleepless
to guard against the threat nearing that seamless
enclosure of azure sky acquired by this *Meccano*
and *Hornby* world. And here, maintaining for *You*
its own brand of sunlight, is lush grass with summers

of flowers, blatant or covert, undyingly profuse
in propaganda fields. Listen: the domestic insects buzz
the industrious drones of their trades. In such a universe
bees blur to hymn and celebrate the absolutes
of land lying loam and rich whose pastoral and friendly trees
adapt their limbs to patriotic gestures.
In their untroubled shade, a modest Church is

pointing a Heaven that only these trees, these villages
deserve and own. Yet, threat is somewhere,
for here Horatian on the foreground grass
are the young men, the devil-may-care freelances
of the sky's regions. Artless, they breathe a purer air
than those among the dusty seats reading an atmosphere
redolent with threat, impending as the structures

of an Auden poem. These are the paladins in sheepskin armour
whose exhaust trails bulletin the empyrean,
scrawling their love-affair with death, whose youthful clamour
blazons just cause. Some lounge in deck-chairs. Another
writes his last letter to a winsome girl. An idyll's reign
is always too good to last. Even in cloudless skies, the obscene
must lie concealed where air already spills the echo

whose dangerous meaning clatters in the klaxons
calling to arms. Mess doorways explode. There is
that galvanising rush of the young knights, at a run
pulling their flying-suits to shape, with laughter hauling on
protective leathers and stirring to war-cry the dull fuss
of trailing thongs, the snick and clash of harness
that marks their sunlit scramble. Here starts that mythical mission

to win the Grail, to stem the waste-land's inroads.
Spitfires and Hurricanes poise a tarmac for ever golden
where an English sun anthems on England's fields,
gilds English trees, pulpits its hallowing trades
on the stones of an English Church. They squadron
to serve such never icons, that never congregation
of winsome girls, blimp Colonels, Rectors, Postmen, old Maids.

2. For Franc Sesec

It was the last album page
of triangle stamps. Schoolroom histories
charted its ritual collisions
of Christendom with Islam, recounted
a Bosnia-Herzegovina somewhere between
grand-guignol and comic opera.
Not much prepares. A coaching Archduke
bursts in Sarajevo. Later, our wirelesses
tuned in to partisans, reprisals.
Newsreel flickered Stukas, Tito.
A tortured coastline breaks, confessing
argosies. Stone marshals mountains.
The sun's Gestapo flogs Dalmatia,
Montenegro. And simmering on
the roadside crucifixes, Christ is
suspended bleeding, somewhere between
sentiment and history, limestone
and blue sky. Ubiquitous as Tito,
the pillbox shrines explode in flowers
and plaster Virgins. *Not much prepares.*

Begunje: the white mansion poised
cool as a convent. There are a thousand
minor crucifixions of trapped flies
in webs mantling privet: a scored
history of walls surviving between
atrocity cells. A leaning triptych
of bullet-broken stakes still stands
to gospel Golgotha. *Not much prepares.*
Apples are speared on thorns and birdsong
stilled by the memory of eagles.

Rifle slung at his back, a soldier
is tying Franc Sesec to a tree. It is
another of those imperative
crucifixions, our century's face
and wound, this final dignity
in history's crumpled suit, that look
somewhere between martyrdom and victory.

Iceberg horns of Alps are bayoneting
Slovenia's sky. *Not much prepares.*
A mason is grinding partisan names
into tank-trap monuments. Between
the gunfire rattle of his chisel
and Christ's wingspan agonies, Germans
play football. History here is blindfold
hostage to a tourist sun wasting
its shadows of stakes and wire across
the English faces crowding pavement bars.

3. Jack Barlow's back-row bulletins.

The Globe

Your Honour, at *The Globe* I first
steamed for her swell. On the newsreel,
the *Graf Spee* scuttled. Weaponry raised,
assaulting cruisers fumbled buttons
of shellburst through a blue blouse. A sly
torpedo unzipped silk and slipped beneath
froth at her bows. Her engines shuddered.
Filaments of her rigging parted
over the blister turrets bulging
their stubby guns. One turbulent heave
shook all her structures and a tremulous
sucking signalled her gone. Close-ups came
of sweating faces looming, fingers
saluting air and that strange victory.

The Palace

Your Honour, at the Palace, stubborn
resistance crumbled. On the newsreel,
Monte Cassino fell. A clumsy
infantry pressed to open up the slopes
and hold the lower landscape's fabric.
Soft flanks gave way and reinforcement
of the encircling cordons stopped. Commandos
scaled bare approaches. Opposition
slackened. A hot advance surrounded
covered emplacements hardly shielding
a deployed division. Unchallenged
shock troops reached their prize. A moaning
siren breathed its surrender. Close-ups
caught panting corporals embracing.

The Roxy

Your Honour, at the *Roxy,* I
learned victory's defeat. On the news, Russians
entered the *Reichstag.* The flags
came down. Supine, the female city
disposed her limbs to that first column
hot to possess her. That military
ravishing by a crude soldiery
was mercenary stuff. No shining
citadel fell. She offered only
an indifferent body that bemoaned
lost politics and rued that enforced
nazi salute she harboured. How much
chocolate buys a girl? Close-ups framed
one blubbering her cheap dishonour.

The Court

Your Honour, what am I doing here
alone in the *Court?* Why these newsreels
of Nuremberg trials? Can peace's
inquisitors in their other laws
weigh wartime's acts? All the evidence
is lies or vain exaggeration.
A Himmler chemistry and a Goering
swagger sits in the flesh. Our ether's
thick with a Goebels' propaganda.
I know them well. The lower ranks obeyed
blurred orders from a higher command.
Who shaped my state? A madman hiding
in an impregnable bunker. Close-up,
one familiar, unregenerate face.

4. A garden of Earthly Delights
(Bosch's triptych: Hell)

i.

We have been here before: such times
as allegory's slim transparencies slither
uselessly, unwitting of metaphor's
skeleton keys. How grammar the mind's
labyrinths, flesh's turbulent animal?
Can tempera breach death's maulings?
Sergeant, where in hell are we?

We have been here before: the Fun House's
Barnum beckoning us to atrocity, to observe
the congealed logarithms of torture,
to see suffering's obscure square roots,
to know the enigma geometries of punishment.
Enter, he says, my vistas of fallen folly.
Sergeant, where in hell are we?

We have been here before: the Freudian
discovering in his collection of grotesques,
in a queer eavesdropping of corruption's taint,
a rotten deeper self. Only a mind fixated,
fascinated by the parasitic purposes
of flesh's economics, so gestures the soul's biology.
Sergeant, where in hell are we?

We have been here before: see now
alchemy's bleak laboratory where tempera
emulsifies a dubiously colloidal
transit through death's membrane to a region
of allotropic existence, a symbiotic
reversal of death in life, a corporal eternity.
Sergeant, where in hell are we?

ii.

We have been here before. Sergeant,
where in hell are we? Are we still
in that trench where a whizzbang exploded?
Is that Wipers burning? (Time's metronome
is ticking.) Are those our sappers? My compass
spins. My binoculars are lensed with blood.
Sergeant, where in hell are we?

We have been here before. Sergeant,
where in hell are we? A blind sun
burns incendiary on tumuli
of bleached bone where trashed anatomies
shape swastika anagrams. Abel's stench myth
brokers corrupted ground. Who made this garden?
Sergeant, where in hell are we?

We have been here before. Sergeant,
where in hell are we? A death-cap mushroom
spawns Hiroshima's skies: in Nagasaki,
fungal contaminations spore the air.
Truman, Stalin and Attlee posture
in Potsdam's nuclear allotment.
Sergeant, where in hell are we?

5. A Swastika Lullaby

Mother, who is the swastika man
raging his moustache evil,
the apocalyptic Chaplin
of Nuremburg's vaudeville?

Hush child, say nothing,
stifle your question.
The monster is speaking
our state's constitution.

Mother, who is the fat man,
the Reichstag's debauched cherub,
Stukaland's Bacchus blown
to blitzkrieg's Beelzebub?

Hush child, take cover,
lie snug in your shelter.
When the black planes drum over,
it is you they search for.

Mother, who is the staring man,
skin stripped to gargoyle who
crows the Inferno's dominion
in a Gothic Esperanto?

Hush child, lie close and still
or his truth's lying refrain,
like an invisible sootfall,
will blacken your brain.

Mother, who is the leaning man,
Hell burning his eyes,
whose Judas posture screams in
Treblinka's atrocities?

Hush child, it is a spook
baring the truth that underlies
our being. You must not look
into such honest eyes.

Mother, who are the cyanide pair
consumed by a flaring passion
of petrol in a bunker?
Where has the swastika gone?

Hush child, say a prayer.
It lives in the minds of men.
Someone has hidden the swastika.
It will turn up again.

Jairmany calling

(William Joyce, Lord Haw Haw, born in Brooklyn. of Irish parents, holder of a British passport for nine months, executed as a traitor on the basis of a questionable and possibly unsound legal judgment.)

Lies are truth's living substance. Why else
is God mad? Why else fact's infertility
and fabulation's force? Metaphor's mystery
rebels the mind's flat countries. I spoke only
the idiot's sagacity, breath's faithless fidelity.

Dishonour is the profoundest honour. Why else
the world's paradox? Why else duality
in words' workings? It is the lexicon's lies
mould the mind's manacles. What language
speaks the unspeakable? Ask Hamburg's Coventries.

Experience is the final innocence. Why else
Eden's mythical truth? Why else infinity
of mind shackled to finite body?
The tongue's prehensile tickle touches silence.
I preached the timeless minute of fame's infamy.

Dishonesty is the heart's honesty. Why else
the rat beneath the skin? Why else the pregnancy
of pride's humility? Only the symbol's soaring
impels clay's inertia. Who was it spoke
the swastika's complex simplicity?

Absurdity is life's logic. Why else
the soul's mangle? Why else this oddity:
faith's earthbound flight in the quisling fixity
of things? What winds the spirit's wind? And who
dictated Nuremberg's impotent potency?

Treachery is the last patriotism. Why else
my bullet's laming kiss? Why else avidity
in my poem's matrix, the doctrine's compactions
outside the dictionary's doldrum? Why such
garbled clarity curing straight's aridity?

Injustice shapes the greatest justice. Why else
the state's corruption? Why else this quiddity:
the legal fiction's fact that shapes mis-shape
into the lived fact's fiction? So they contrive
my nine-month passport to eternity.

My end is my beginning. Why else
the blinding light? Why else this subtlety
of freedom's noose? Silence's noise must make
air as my last and firmest footing for
my drop's leap into a future history.

Memento Mori.

Memento Mori

‘Not many like my voice, but everyone hears
my jargon in the end. For you it might be
my sales chat on your mobile touting time-shares
you can’t resist in some uncharted country.
I hide in machines that speak your weight
just as your *Mass* assumes its capital. I inhabit
the lift’s robot lips, the monotone that says
‘Your door is closing.’ You will hear my dialect,
waiting alone in some darkened station,
that blur from another platform’s tannoy breaching
your ears with its message that the last train
to nowhere you can imagine is now approaching.’

Dead Seas

‘Dead seas aren’t geographical. Tides swell
in the mind’s craters, swilling their flotsam
of myth or allegory or a parable.
Paul Nash stared at this sea and spent his time
painting aeroplanes. I didn’t see any.
Once, we had fishers of men, though that’s
bibles ago. They told some story
of how their mate, with bits of bread and sprats
netted five thousand. But fishermen’s tales
are fishermen’s tales. Sprats swell to mackerels
and mackerels bloat to aeroplanes or whales,
swarming the mind’s seas with their parables.’

Tardis

'Welcome aboard my Tardis. Here you
can buy the map to guide you to the place
that sells maps. We arrange transport to
vain hope, defeated dreams. We personalise
your bottle holding the last blue smoke aroma
of lost love's cigarette. For the real losers,
our shelves are groaning with the nostalgia
of *I did it My Way* and we take orders
for records of *Je ne regrette rien* for those
who regret everything. We charge no fees
for the use of this contraption's limbo space
as echo chamber for your world's failed promise.'

Actuary

'Let Madam Sosostris nurse her cold in peace.
Forget her silly deck. Ignore her presence.
Your fortune is already told and there is
no chance that the shuffle and random occurrence
of cards can correspond to what you are
or what portends. In every horoscope,
I am in the hand you are dealt and your future
is augured in my bones. So go and grope
your divination from some sad Sosostris:
you will pay her in vain. Whatever you do
- no matter how you try to play the ostrich -
I wait within you. I have always been you.'

v. Semtex

'I am the bone to which all other bones
have bent. I am plastic. My grammar is
I will. Words wear my terrorist explosives
and I have primed a fissile tongue to fuse
religions, to make gods and oppose them other.
I chew lexicons to put the slime behind
and melt the world's solid shape. My lips stutter
sin's documentaries, tell each episode
of salvation's soap. I scream outrage
in time's unhearing amphitheatre. *I will.*
Language within a world that lacks language
moulds me the semtex architect of hell.'

NARRATIVE

All my Dead Uncles

1.

'All Your dead Uncles.' Their images beamed –
Albert and Walter, James and John and Henry -
from sepia photographs unframed,
a cracked and yellowing rosary
fixed by a shrivelled Sellotape and forming
their rank on George's mirror. *Puisieux* and *Serre.*
Fell on the Somme. I knew the chiselling
of names in gilded stone, the year,
nineteen sixteen, a pigeon-woman's songs.
But better this, their soiled, immutable
immortality, their frozen starings
from the etched mirror, shaping a suitable
patriotism. Bullet-belted, drawn
in khaki smiles and not that long from falling,
Albert and Henry, Walter, James and John,
smiling with not much time for smiling.
'A hole big as an egg-cup in his head,
young Walter died in my arms.' George moved
in landscapes where his khaki youth had stayed
and my dead Uncles of his memory survived.
Water was running high. From George's, we
could hear the upstream rumble of the weir
marching its froth battalions endlessly
in regiments through the winter air.

2.

In George's house below the spluttering weir,
stuck to his mirror hanging at a lean,
Albert and Henry, James and John and Walter,
all my dead Uncles marched its garden scene
etched into glass. In a thin cartoon,

parasol women kept eternal guard,
hollyhock lances speared a gilded sun
and in unlikely trees an unlikely bird
carolled a scratch. Two symmetrical
cellophane butterflies on suckers clung
to a reflecting sky. *'That mirror's all*
I ever kept of what he left me. Something
Young Walter loved. Look at it, lad - a poem in
itself.' George boasted with no diffidence,
proposing his aesthetic implication
as something I was sure to countenance.
The pigeon-woman's croon, the bloody *Somme,*
Walter and Henry, James and John and Albert
were emblems impotent to guard or damn
his mirror's mediocre tact and art.
The river wheeling woundedly and slow
carried detritus, scum making its march
in broken ranks. High water had bombed through
its reaches to storm the bridge's arch.
George dragged my childhood out of humdrum,
constructing khaki myths for my retrieve:
Puisieux, Serre, the trenches and the grim
mess of their ends. *'All bloody five*
dead in a week. Young Walter looked like you.
Died in my arms.' In my mind's shambles,
his mirror fossils their bravado
and their permanence, all my dead Uncles.

3.

Cousin Tom's mimicry: *'Poor Walter died.*
And Henry, Albert, John and James...'
With his thin face and frame, he imitated
George's stump walk and psalmodies.
Without a cap, he hinted George's, wore
invisibly the stained fag drooping slack

on George's lip. *'Piss Puisieux and Serre.*
bugger his Somme.' Tom put his mark
on names I'd learned as rosary of a cult
more sensitive, the trench orison
that Tom, ungulled, heard only as some fault,
the scratchings of an ageing gramophone.
Later, with George beside the swollen river,
Albert and Henry, James, John, Walter, all
marched broken between us where Tom's mirror
tainted their image, ordered our squall.
In George's garden by the weir, we quarrelled
where, at our side, sheathed leaves of lilac
strained to a disappointing spring. A cold,
and spluttering morning saluted a fleck
of sun in a grey sky. In the wet meadows
beyond the weir, the weak light flared its sour
illumination and the white asbestos
of football stands was briefly golden. *'Your*
sod of a cousin Tom's done this,' George said,
marshalling yet again John, James and Henry,
Albert and Walter, for ever egg-cup holed,
all my dead Uncles marching khaki,
parading in the river's swill downstream.
Above us, the weir churned its April spate
in regiments of froth, their column
broken by mortar winds along the straight.

4.

'Caught anything?' George was loading
battles and blood into his query.
Wilf, oil-skinned, had caught George descending
to stall his fishing in the river bay.
Much comradeship involved the lower air.
'Wilf fought in France,' George said. I'd known.
We turned towards the splutter of the weir.

Wilf had progressed, was George's implication
into the dry, self-gratifying, peace-
ful whims of age, while he had stayed to choose
politics' battleground. *'They call this place
Moscow because of me.'* The empty phrase
cracked acres of time. I'd heard his same
expression years ago, a boastful paean
before the photographs and, mocking him,
Tom had stabbed accurately at his tone
for names I'd held in sentimental creed.
Later, I watched George posture, stand
by the rails of the weir as he proposed
himself, when young, dead Walter's friend -
He looked like you do now - Albert and James,
Henry and John, grey hair against grey sky.
Tom had been right to stab. *'They call this place
Moscow because of me.'* My sympathy
for George had shrivelled. *Puisieux* and *Serre,*
the pigeon-woman's songs, the *Somme*,
Albert and Henry, James and John and Walter:
he marshalled an appeal but it was time
to raise them in a morning's colder light.
'Caught anything?' I mocked his charlatan
postures with Wilf. Tom had been right
to stab. George spun deflated for me then.

5.

Fitful sun pecking the gilded grooves
of *Puisieux* and *Serre, Fell on the Somme,*
lit pigeons on the graveyard's drives
near the stump Cenotaph. Albert and John,
Henry and James: George traced the stone
East Lancashires. *'Young Walter looked
like you.'* The pigeon-woman's croon
was with me then but George had tracked

to nearer things. *'Tom Morton's made a mess.*
One bloody woman and he's winded.
A pig's ear of a marriage.' Time to recognise
an old man anxious to be reminded
by any blandishment at my disposal
that he had stayed the four years of a war
and more than Tom had had his fill
of women. *'When we were over there*
we didn't go without.' The scum platoons
formed ranks along the river's shelf,
swilled slowly down in punk battalions,
and open order, passing the Cenotaph,
the weir's conscripted infantry,
detritus bubbles parading bladder
regiments on the move, a bubble army,
khaki impostures on the water.

'Apres la guerre finee
Soldiers Anglais partee,
Beaucoup M'amselles dans la family way.
Apres la guerre pitee.....'

I hawked the pigeon-woman's song and he
took it with savour. With it, I urged mistake
for flattery but offered a trenched mockery
without commitment. If he chose to look
no further than its surface geography,
it gestured what he had wanted, lands
to conjure adulation. *'When you try,*
you're the only one who understands.'
Sudden sunlight flecked the graves,
regilding momentarily his stone
East Lancashires, their fading names:
Albert and Henry, Walter James and John.

6.

The river marching slow, in single shots,
grey water lapped the military weir,
attrition weather scorched the bankside flats,
trenching the waterline. A squad of star-
lings squabbled over bread. George lay
beneath the butterflies of Walter's glaze-
necropolis, remaking loonily
his khaki myths. The pigeon-woman's wraiths
crooned for him there, spilling the words
that carried for him the flux memory
of my dead Uncles, the bauble-lads
of *Puisieux* and *Serre*: Albert and Henry,
James and John, relentless as the scums
he told them: Walter who never died -
he looked like you do now - reclaimed his arms,
a hole big as an egg-cup in his head.
The river's slowing march had paced his mind.
Stagnant detritus there had overpiled
in spawny clumps. Capricious wind
flirted the clusters upstream. Then a shrivelled
and sudden, contorted anger marked
his mood. He jerked to mouth accusingly –
'*Henry and Walter, James and John and Albert* –'
marshalled their memory to damn me.
*'I was your friend. Young Walter looked like you.
Tom Morton made us enemies, the bastard.'*
Then sank to ride the river's sluggish flow
towards them, old and exhausted..

7.

In George's house by the spluttering weir,
stuck to his mirror, hanging at a lean,
six photographs. *East Lancashire,*

he'd written on each one. The crinoline
ladies, hollyhocks and that sharp bird among
etched trees commanded the frame
and of the khaki images that clung,
we carried out the last. Five chiselled names
I knew in polished stone, but knew this grander,
and sepia deathlessness. Six cracked and faded
photographs had petrified a bland or
wondering, glazed but still unjaded
patriotism. Bullet-belted, shrined
in thin and khaki smiles, not far from falling,
unthinking, ignorant and blind,
five smiled with not much time for smiling.
The river sliding downstream, dully,
a light wind rippling in clearer patches,
cumbersome regiments of froth moved slowly
bridgeward, veered in gusts between the houses.
Bushed and intricate, contorted squads
slithered the river's central path,
swilled slowly downstream, punk armadas
under a fading sunshine, past the Cenotaph.
I watched them drop the last of George away,
counted nine mourners, heard intoned,
with not much vigour, hope or urgency
words he rejected, watched them hymn the God
he'd never found. Earth that should have smacked
ritually at his coffin was a pinch
of finest to be found. With decency and tact
they killed what he had been. Judged to the inch,
we posted him respectably away.
I had mixed feelings for him then, played games
with hidden grief, added in mockery
another to those five chiselled names.

8.

On the stump Cenotaph's architectures,
a generation too removed for pity
scrawled its bewilderments. Dead fusiliers
wore camouflage where an obscene graffiti
saluted cruder loves and posturings
than theirs. From fluted pillars, pigeons
at their dung trades, grouted the chisellings,
turning to shit my Uncles' gilded runes.
The weir in winter flood, its boom
built bubble monuments, toppling the spate
into a floodgate swill, landscaped a *Somme*
of scum exhaustion labouring the flat.
Daily and loonily she limped the rail
beside the Cenotaph, distributing
manna in pinches. Around her, a swell
of bucking pigeons scrummed to her song.
She threw a spray of crumbs, hauling a drogue
of hopelessness in her bewildered rave,
cursing the birds she fed, a monologue
that hymned her crazy no-man's land of love.
And there, beneath the Cenotaph, George spun
back in those silted chisellings that will
embalm and emblemise him better than
emotion for the men they name. Yet still,
let me recount them, all my dead Uncles, James,
Albert and Henry, John, Walter who died –
He looked like you do now – in George's arms,
a hole big as an egg-cup in his head.

Wolves

1. *What can I do for you?*

I had meant to look up Buckley, walked
once more along the river where the weir
marshals froth armies skating the water
towards and then beyond the football ground.
Drizzle had sharpened the flow, persistent enough
to flatten and re-regiment the scum
of khaki flotsam moving downstream,
dissolving to swill, a discoloured scarf,
on the river's flow. My interruption
of Buckley's light caused him to turn and signal,
not then in recognition but as casual
and undirected, maybe hopeful indication
that I might want to see him. Then a lame
recollection crossed his face. His posture
and the taut muscles of the neck were
still with him: his tall and lumbering frame
was fatter but not much clumsier
than it remained held in my memories.
There were photographs of his playing days
on the wall behind him, mostly the blur
of action shots, mainly the local press
where he remained, poised permanently
as the man I remembered, perpetually
clumsy in movement and self-conscious
when made to pose. Their impact was to endow
a wasting nostalgia for a time's pretence
that carried shards of a lost innocence.
Wolves stalked me then. *'What can I do for you?'*

2. The Language of my kind

Photographs on his wall poised older sides,
in teams that only another generation
might have remembered, though I had known
myself among the later ones, the lads
posturing unremembered under glass,
provoking agonistically the language
of once my kind, enshrining the gauge
and social dimensions of our class.
My mind was drawn to fading images:
mean winters in the depressed thirties,
the flat-cap brigades cramming the tiers
of terraces for Saturday's release.
Losing eyes stared and I remembered
games that I'd seen when younger, still in thrall
to players and teams. In my recall
they played to groans and roars, never the breed
or sort of men who valued neat applause
or any recognition of finesse, the hardly clever
carpenters of ball-play and rarely ever
its cabinet makers. I knew their cause,
men trapped in caste and time by grease-licked hair,
bull-necks shaved convict high. They wore,
from boots to faces, the insignia
of what they were, workaday pros and never
the moneyed amateurs, the shabby infantry
and never the Lancers. I looked into that gallery
and found what I had known I'd gather:
the language of my kind. I sought again
its nouns and verbs, its burly grammar
and wondered if I might know any more
its shapes and dialects. Wolves stalked me then.

3. *Not a cup, not a medal*

'What can I do for you?' What could he do?
He could bring back to me the taste of the past:
could shrivel my abstinence to nothing:
could bring back a dead and vanished time
in the colours I had once known:
could torture and contort a time itself.
He turned away. *'He was some bloody player'* -
acknowledging the needless namelessness
of his remark, by nodding, to fix my guess,
towards the photograph of Naylor.
'Wasn't he class? Just what I wish we had
to top this bloody league.' Then suddenly,
hope shifted to regret. I felt some pity
and maybe understood his changing mood,
and hidden circumstances. *'Half my life*
with buggerall to show for it. No showcase.
Never a cup or medal. Hardly a piece
of bloody paper. Is there no fairness? When I've
settled my heart on winning this league? I want
to see a bloody cup, the first I've ever won,
sit there this season. This is my one
and only chance.' He gestured his intent
with little hope for its reality,
towards his crowded desk where I could see
no room for his imagination's trophy.
Wolves stalked me then. His vulnerability
was all too obvious. *'Maybe,'* I said.
'Maybe.' The thought harnessed my mind
that fate was just but hardly ever kind.
Then it was time to go....

4. Wolves

He understood the terms of my withdrawal,
staring across the ground, a mist's occasion
laying its tissue-paper on the afternoon,
a fine obscurity beginning to crawl
from its nest in the river's confine,
beginning to digest the terraces that lay
around the pitch. *'Better be on your way.*
Just like you did before.' I think it was then
I recognised the pain in his disquiet
and in its repetition. More than a need
for trophies. Afterwards I deduced -
though nothing was ever said about it -
that he had known his state, that he had guessed
what was consuming him. '*Time I was off.'*
Wolves stalked me then. I saw the wolf
within him. '*Look after yourself,'* he said.
'I always did.' I guessed at his defeat
'You always did. We all knew that.' He might
have learned new ironies. I knew the bite
of my own and different wolf and felt it
chewing within me. The pitch was obscure,
deserted, and I remembered its weight
and sogginess as I moved across it
towards the open turnstile in the corner.
While our strange salutations had continued,
the mist had levitated further from the river,
a light wind shifting its fragility over
and through the terraces of the ground.
obscuring now the distant goal. *Wolves*
stalked me then.

Team Photographs

1. Team Photographs

George led me to the wall where thirty-one
photographs in black and white proposed
thirty-one seasons of a side that never won
anything. Young and brash, we colonised
in callow ranks, athletically transfixed,
a team without distinction. First, he stared,
not at myself but at Hugh Naylor, poised
arms folded, head erect in an assured
self-confidence in some earlier team.
George spoke, voice loaded with reproach,
'You know the story, that man did me harm.'
He moved to point my later photograph -
'You're sitting where he sat' - struck visually
to shape our present quarrel. Seasons later, young,
I poised the same null landscape over me,
the slowly vitiating and corroding
townscapes of a time and mood less innocent
than I or our young faces had supposed.
Black and white stripes posed celluloid assent.
Petrified, agonistic, we advertised
two different seasons of a side that never won
anything. Upland behind us were
the marches of a landscape I had known,
the blind and narrow town under the moor,
the pattern of the mean, ascending streets
that fashioned us. George pointed Naylor
and myself, wearing corrupting industries,
complicit in that landscape's weather.

2. Some metaphors for the Ground

From a turn in the road, the town lies
biting the moor's flank. Street fingers feel
and grope the fell. Chapel chimneys
tickle its thigh, the jugular canal
arteries through emptied mills. The decayed
white of asbestos football stands unleagued
commemorates a side that specialised
in relegation. The pitch preens, grassed
to jewel, in the armpit of this dross
den under the moor. Chapels fail
in bids for re-election: factories
smoke on the transfer list where football
wears faces ripe to move from innocence
in seasons of a side that never won
anything, sliding a limbo dance
from league to league within its worn
tatter of terraces. Folded arms
and fossil grins commemorate a side
- hardened old pros in their last games
and aspirant lads, some of them on the road
to higher leagues - a schizophrenia
matched in results. The stand's asbestos
leans monument to lost sides that wear
thirty-one seasons of a team that tows
its past to swell the grudge offence that sits
the streets and alleyway of this blind
tent under the moor where relegation waits
to stalk us in seasons not yet played.

3. Manager: Arthur Buckley

Manager: Arthur Buckley. It proclaimed
one of life's losers. Empty and likeable,

the world's fool, still my friend, unchanged
except his age and girth. He'd stayed the affable
man I remembered. The full-back features,
the swollen, heavy muscles of the neck,
retained their trademark. His body was
fuller but not much clumsier. He took
pride in old photographs damp had spoiled
with emulsion's bombs. Some were past teams,
some, action fragments scissored from old
newspapers, some gripped by their frames,
in postures fixing the naivete
that held him gullible, the easy butt
of more worldly games. He could betray
my secret ridicules to grief, a target
making my blame ambiguous for one
of life's persistent losers. *'In this game
for twenty years, what have I ever won?
No medals. Never a cup.'* I pitied him,
not his incompetence or lack of prizes,
but all he never knew, his dull goodness.
His world would need new rules and referees
for him to kiss its cups or wave its trophies.

4. Landlord of The World's End

Our meeting was deliberate enough,
myself and Naylor, near *The World's End*,
his newest strumpet, perching its fief
in moor and car-park. The accident
that scraped his wife to leglessless showed
no surface scratch. Together, we climbed to
the moorhead. Beneath us, the town splayed
its legs in the offence of streets we knew,
that shaped simplicity within the space
our ignorance permitted. Naylor spoke
derisively -*'An arsehole of a place'*-

turning to gloat his *World's End's* wantonness
slutting the moor. *'It's mine. I always said*
I'd have it. Something sodlike crushes' -
he pointed -*'our sort down there. I made*
certain of better.' Across the moor
his painted excrescence winked. I guessed
that there, Agnes might cuddle the lure,
of paper-back romances. Some malice paced
my own derision. *'How's Agnes been?'*
'She mentions you. Usually that night
she danced with you. She used to carry on.'
Despair or some once admiration might
have prompted him. He knew my jibe -
'There's always Alice, can't be wasted'-
With equal irony he brushed aside
my own. *'Which of us is the bastard?'*

5. Four conversations

i. Alice Buckley at The World's End

I knew the mock refinement of her voice
dismissing me as salesman when she said,
'He isn't here -' squawking her compromise
noises, not remembering me. *'Did*
Hughie know you were coming? Are you new?'
The photograph behind her on the wall
was one I'd seen before. On it the row
of losing faces bubbled on a swell
of town and moor, eleven on their way
to winning nothing. *'Mister Naylor's there -'*
she pointed where he sat. *'He used to play*
for England when he was a footballer.
He's out today.' She queened in his affairs
and thought she knew my business. I knew hers.

ii. Landlord of The Dog

'And so, you're back among us -' On his wall,
the serried photographs were spanning
thirty-one seasons of a side that fell
steadily through the leagues. Shorts too long
and heavy boots were ranked in black and white
striped shirts, luminous under the hill.
He nodded to me. *'Now Hugh Naylor's got*
The World's End for himself. Tarted it up to pull
the gin trade.' 'Does he get it?' He laughed
at that. My thought had been the vacancy
of car park. *'Gets it alright,'* he said.
'A bit more than he should, I've heard. Let's say,
visitors who might be better off
home with their husbands. Your sort of stuff.'

iii. Agnes Naylor at The World's End

'And as for Alice, couldn't you see
I've known about her playing Hughie's queen.
Couldn't you see I knew?' I saw that she
had needed to tell me and had always been
ungulled. *'I'm not so foolish. And I've known*
about the others.' I looked for spite,
some spring of sourness in her. I saw none.
'His little weakness.' Then I knew that she
she had never been opponent of his games
but agent and entrepreneur and they
were gestures of a sort, her schemes
a kind of love, maybe compassion.
And then she struck. *'You got your ration.'*

iv. Landlord of The Dog

On ruined and recorded landscapes, those
old photographs, apocryphal, still wore
in agonistic, schizophrenic rows,
past disillusion and endeavour.
For his own ironies, he pointed
Buckley and Naylor, team-mates in a side
on the way down. *'You know that Arthur's resigned*
today? Poor bloody Arthur,' he said.
'A job for Naylor then?' Maliciously,
I fed the snippet to him, let him wind
his answer. *'Well, he does one job for Buckley.*
Too much to give him another.' And,
outside my irony and unaware,
he was still laughing. I'd had my share.

6. A rhetoric for Naylor's penitence

'I've had enough of Agnes. You can't tell
what I've put up with.' The scalding shower
that he endured, I found unbearable.
'That whole bloody business with the car -'
He didn't finish nor did he need to finish.
I knew about the car, but better,
its acid preludes. Agnes had danced to squash
her sour recriminations in my ear,
resentment fouling the night. Arthur
and Alice Buckley shared the table.
Someone took photographs. Naylor,
quarrelsome, drunk and incapable,
half-killed her on the way home, although
he stayed unscathed. She lost her legs. That was
the business with the car. *'I've had enough,*
it's too much in the end.' In places
the penance shower missed, he raised

lather to conceal confessional.
'I want what going but I can't get past
Agnes. It's left me with buggerall.
I never wanted more than a fairish ration.
Just some sort of relief and mainly
what you were getting. Some alleviation.
My life is skint.' That was his only
occasion of complaint, the one time
I saw the hurt that squatted in his centre
in those loquacious seconds when he came
clean in the assault of scalding water.

7. Those old photographs

'We've had the albums out. The old ones -'
Thirteen at table, a white cloth's furl.
a glaze of sharp magnesium hardens
apostle faces. '*Your red-haired girl'* –
Buckley, blinks central, haloed by an arch
of window: car headlights contour the fell.
His palm lies upward, somewhere an ash-
tray, wafers and red wine. We smile
in dresses and suits. Randy Agnes,
fixing that flash in virgin white, betrays
little except her smirk for Alice
at that strange supper. Her gesture stays.
Naylor leans towards Buckley. His pose
mocks innocence. That pregnant girl,
now George's complaint, at that time knows
nothing, although my wafer lust was all
bursting for Agnes. By far the best-
looking, and randy and available,
who, as we danced, salacious, promised
all that I wanted. Her tongue was full
of spite, a jealousy and resentment
tricking her flesh's intention to splay

her readiness for a dance more urgent.
On the drive home, he scraped her legs away,
and that was that, our dance undone.
All that we proposed, smiling behind
the modelled cloth, the wafers and the wine,
the smoking ash-tray, never happened.
Captured prophetic, Arthur Buckley
beams innocence where Hugh Naylor
postures the eternal judas-lie.
Alice smiles enigmatic, seems to stare
at truth on or beneath Agnes's dress.
'We opened the old albums. Stuff to shame
you at your antics. Touching up Agnes.
And that lass you shagged. What was her name?'

8. Housewarming

'No holy water with it?' I'd never known
Naylor to water whisky. *'Where's the tap?*
I'm driving.' I recalled a time he'd driven
drunker. As children, we'd known the shape
of houses like this, once were dough in these
unleavened terraces and knew the cage
of their yards, their rooms' geographies.
His water was charade to camouflage
words for my ear. We moved towards the bare
space of a stone-flagged kitchen. *'Arthur*
won't last. I don't know what they've told her.'
Our host's housewarming laughter cut across
his concern. *'She knows'* – he eyed the regions
where Alice stood – *'she hasn't said. It's cancer.'*
It shaped his awed confession. The kitchen's
cold penanced it. *'It's only a year*
they give him. I hope he never knows.'
Which flesh or whose betrayal Arthur ought
never to know I never knew. The tap spun

under his hand and icy water spat,
rumbling piped to blur his confession,
although he kept his glass an inch outside
its splutter. *'Some circumstances when
camouflage matters,'* I think he said.

9. Apples for a dying man.

'He loves to sit among his apple trees.'
Alice told spreading orchards to cheer
his illness. *'Out in his summer-house.'*
Arthur was watching from his lawn's square
a match of wind and bloom. Six lean trees
were losing badly in a framed enclosure
of concrete, on that poor pitch, for his
last season's game. Fragile, immature
blossom was being kicked to defeat.
His hair had greyed, cheeks sunk and thinned,
the bull-neck lost its force. He nodded at
the trees in flimsy bloom. *'If you come round
to see us later on, I'll give you some fruit.'*
Wind butting urban sunshine culled
unfruitful seed. Sucking at bottled
stout for his health, he raised his glass to pour,
clumsily, spilling a liberal froth that rode
towards the trees. Bottle and flower
conflicted in his mood. *'Guinness is good.
What did I ever win but relegation?'*
Seen from his shelter, the match had run
almost to its result. The bitter question
blew from his mouth and like the froth was borne
downwind to join the fallen blossom that,
once promising succulence, now lay
among the dead leaves and the birdshit,
latent to spur a richer life. Maybe.

10. A threnody for dancings done

'It's a long time since we were dancing –'
Agnes cadenced her tentative phrase
towards me, unsure but still causing,
as she had intended to cause,
recall of a time when we had had
hopes of a different dancing as we danced.
That night she spent her venom in tirade
condemning Naylor. Now she evidenced
her need that I might still remember
our conspiracy. On the way home,
drunken and angry, he broke the car and her.
That night, she lost her legs. That quarrelsome
night of our dancing brought back to me
her offers of a more urgent dancing,
recalled her acid mood and finally
her features, finely beautiful, parading
her crudest promises to my ear.
I searched now with new ironies for a face
once beautiful but grown angular,
distorted, and that night's ugly voice
the gentlest that I knew. She had been
urgent then, queer lewdness in her tone,
projecting it as her game's design.
And afterwards, as he drove her home,
that cruel, crippling business when
he broke the car and her. My thought hung
on the dry spaces of her life since then.
'It seems a long time since we were dancing –'

11. Alice Buckley: Blackberry and Apple pie

He can have his home-grown apples with them –'
She poured the berries slowly and they ran
like blood in an enamelled sunstream,
pulsed liquid and uncurdled, out of one
bag into another. *'Yes, it's cancer.'*
Thin plastic squealed where her fingers fought.
'*Blackberry and apple pie.'* Her anger
held all malignant nature in garotte.
She screwed the neck and with deliberation
tightened it, to burst the berries' blood.
Ribbons of juice spurted a profusion
for vicious lubricant to her mood.
'With his own apples - 'Jewelled sun lurched
on fruit debauched, bulging as she strained
to a scorpion anger where she arched
and stung herself. Under her blenched hand,
swollen and tight, the red membrane burst
to spurt slush fruit. I heard her scream
of anger the distending bag released.
'What use are fucking blackberries to him -'

12. A fireplace with a copper hood

'Tell Naylor I know now.' A tongued fire
was blazing, brawling a copper throat.
His face, reflected, was a skull and wore
a medieval mask of death. A bright
scutter of ash shifted the firelight within
its indentations. His bitter words
swelled in a metal cheek's emblazon
on moquette. He slid dull eyes towards
team photographs, the lost sides askew
over the hooded fire, where in the line,
himself and Naylor grinned the spew

of rotting stands. *'What did we ever win?
It's all a bloody cheat.'* The firelight was
scraping a face ridged by the moquette's
impress. *'I know that now.'* His braces
drooped slackly on frail shoulders, trousers
gaping where once his belly had
swollen the waist. A bluster of wind
was sucking elastic tongues renewed
from the flat fire. *'Tell Naylor I found
out in the end.'* Which flesh and blood
treacheries he'd solved I never knew.
Such words he howled beside that copper hood
were all time's relegations blowing through
poor sides unleagued, shaping our bleak
metaphor of narrow streets, the sour
untruths of chapels, the god we make
from images of fear at what we are.

13. Requiem

Thirty-one photographs still enshrine
those sides unfutured in their team rows,
screwing to private relegation.
Asbestos stands, decaying, still enclose
the jewel pitch. Mills slouch degenerate
under the moor. Heads erect, arms folded,
agonistic, we commemorate
thirty-one seasons of a limbo slide,
thirty-one seasons of flesh and blood's
persisting treacheries. Buckley's cheer,
if it survives, must simplify new sides
in alien leagues. Along with Naylor,
I share ungrounded fixtures, played
away from home. More than the cameras'
coincidences fix us among greed
mills and chapels where our faces

stare into time not innocent from time
not innocent. We posture, the bruised,
legitimate offspring of our noisome
camp on the moor, propose the crude
bible of matches lost in its streets,
acknowledge as our father the god
of games where relegation waits
to stalk us in seasons not yet played.

Love on the Moor

1. Joe Anderson

What witnesses? I call the ballock sun,
its banded light bounced from the canal fence
to testify. The randy cats sunning on
brown linoleum hold telling evidence.
Witnessing what? Joe Anderson among
his hunks of ripe and rotten meat to breed
maggots for fishing where, too long
confined, the particles explode
in iridescence, new bluebottles boom
and splinter in confusion at the light,
clouding the level sunshine of the room.
Do I subpoena witnesses to that?
Joe moved with a superb dexterity,
stalked bluebottles, cupping his hand
pelota-shape, to strike out suddenly
and hold them in his palm docile and stunned.
What witnesses? I call the willow-herb
raping the corrugated outhouse roof.
The cats at randy picnic in the yard,
if they had time, would offer certain proof.
Witnessing what? Dexterously he wound,
holding them unconscious and unbroken,
a hair about them. To the other end
he used to tie a small and banal slogan.
On summer days the layered air was hung
with his late captives and their droning weight.
Each hauled its trite but miracle drogue
through spaces of the still and even light.
Guinness is Good or *Beer is Best* was all
that he, Your Worship, managed in that sphere,
less sharp in mind than in that physical

talent he brought perfected from nowhere.
What witnesses? I call the ballock sun
to testify. I call the randy cats,
the raping willow-herb, Joe Anderson.
Dare I subpoena witnesses to that?
It was another climate and that sun
went black. The randy cats defected. Rusts
blighted the willow-herb. The bannered drone
of flies is hypothetical and wastes
in my mind's prairies. Joe Anderson
cancered and died. *The defence rests.*

2. Spring Song

Wakening spring's assault and psalter,
larks rang their bursting business of the fell,
plovers possessed a pulsing sun, the air
held singing distances for new growth's swell.
It was that day, crest piled on crest,
nascent earth's anthem for the spring,
with spearing tendrils of fine grass
and pent life driving, burgeoning.
The road, in the pulse of sun achieved
light's asphalt distances and realms of air,
married a trumpet light, the nuptial wind
swung rituals in aisles of looping wire.
That fullness burgeoned to a bleak excess.
A black discordancy, a breaking,
waited to breach the sun's largesse,
remap the contours of emergent spring.

3. Incident

Boys found, bird nesting on the April moor,
near where we lay, a hand-grenade.
Larks rose and fell. We heard the squeal of fear,

the dull explosion's echo. Someone 'Dead,'
was shouting on the ridge. And then, the men
returning with the body and the wastrel
upthrust of larks, soaring in spring's momen-
tum, charred moor grass stinking in my nostril.
Above us, suddenly where we lay,
black larks cascaded, climbing broken air
in flights unconsummated over the boy
with blown-off hands. And then that other,
that demon boy, white-legged, long-shorted howled
along the ridge. Larks black as time, but older,
fiercer than spring's explosion, held
his cry in scorn. Over the rim of the moor
we saw him lurch. *'Dead,'* he was shouting.
Black-haired, he wore thick glasses and larks hung
black at his head, charred grass detonating
black at his feet. '*Dead,'* he was shouting.

4. Love Song

It was that living day of the fell's grace,
the burst moor's celebration of the spring,
with spearing tendrils of fine grass,
a pent life nascent, burgeoning.

'Tell me about Joe Anderson,' she said.
I might have told the sun, its light
dancing in sibilants of acid
in half-litre beakers, the jewelled weight

of flies towing the miracle drogues
of *Beer is Best* and *Guinness is Good.*
I might have told the catalogues
of what she meant to me. I never did.

His hair was black, that demon boy. He wore
bottle-bottom glasses. Black larks hung
about his head and the charred moor
exploded at his feet. *'Dead,'* he was shouting.

I might have told the willow-herb's decay.
'Tell me about Joe Anderson,' she said.
I might have told the cats, maybe imply
that I loved her. I never did.

5. My Demon Boy

Boys hunting curlew eggs were moving where
remnants of ammunition dumps lie on
the fell's flank. We heard the dull explosion.
In that disastrous telling, he comes over
the ridge of the moor, my golem boy. He wears
the shock of his black hair, those thick-lensed
bottle glasses. '*Dead,'* he is shouting, *'Dead.'*
He is more and less than human. He carries,
outside my understanding, some echo of the moor's
past mystery. Something arcane and mordant
comes with him. Black larks are crescent
about him where the explosion's rumours
shudder the pendulum. *'Dead. He's blown
his bloody hands off.'* His bottle-lenses
gleam in an impossible light, burnt grasses
explode unreal in that manifestation
of the buried primitive, the witch knowing.
I remember running through nascent bracken
to *The World's End's* white isolation.
I recall my impatient waiting and shouting,
an urgent searching for some alarm,
until the door was opened and my reason,
half-understood by a sleepy young woman
in a black dress, who raises her white arm

in sunlight. And then the telephone
that brought an ambulance. Men stretchered down
the body from the moor, lurched through uneven
and tussocked grasses. I have no vision
throughout that time, of the black-haired boy.
He fills no space, might never have existed
except as some once spectral fragment shaped
by the moor's numinous unreality.
I have carried his phantom presence,
punk priest of an otherness, febrile,
my Lazarus in that explosion's quarrel
with the pendulum's normalities….

6. Ending

The evidence of failure lies condign
about me now, shaping the algebraics
of the recalled event. The armoured trucks
of history's quarryings rust overthrown.
Testudo by the ruined railhead's lines,
they shape unpatterned phalanxes, the ghost
unfunctioning machines, marking some lost,
uncomprehended battle. Rusted cranes,
skeleton predators, poise their threats.
Rust's kissing sabotage seduced
and half a century ago, unmanned
the iron on the fell. Now lattice throats
eat only the wind. Since cash's stall,
the moor took back its own, claiming again
the pillaged slopes. '*You wanted this to happen.*'
Among rust iron, she forged a rougher metal
to ravage our slope and shuttered down
piled stone beside her, breaching its wall
to bare its hidden and once integral
architectures to the air's corruption.
Then she held a fragment big as her fist,

to strike at her broadening belly.
'I want it dead.' 'Dead.' And with that sally,
an older language plagued the moor to twist
a thumbscrew time. For seconds he was there
in the fell's resonance, my incarnation.
His bottle-bottom glasses glint arcane,
my demon boy, my golem nightmare
of the moor's mordant will. He brings with him
the witch-knowing, some spectral and tissue
shard of existence. *'I'll make it rue
the life you gave it.'* Her breath rasped from
the vigour of her blow, striking to hide,
with physical pain, a different anguish.
I knew no code to sublimate or diminish
her wilful self-destruction. Wind raked
the disembowelled ridges. Further below,
cold reservoirs forged wrinkled iron
and where the moor still swelled his malediction
my demon boy still rampaged. By then, I knew
the nuances and deceptions of
his damnable and damning identity.
that for so many years has haunted me,
my mirror and myself.....

7. Love on the Moor

Iron and stone contending in the grab
and gouge of quarries wounding the moor
made backdrop to that ending. She tore a web,
complex and labyrinthine as our warfare,
its filaments patterning the cavities
of a wall's decay. Near us, gossamer
linked the rusting trucks. She broke their ties,
numerous as nerves, made metaphor,
in her destruction of their delicacy,
for our disease. Around us and between us,

wrecked membranes of the spiders' industry
told the fragility of webs. Such surgeries
of their transparent, intricate ligament
signalled the warp and weft of our complaint.

You couldn't have phoned from here

1.

The white car, still warm-bonneted, was all
the car park held. I guessed its driver
the woman in broken light beside the bar.
'Ellen's in charge,' she said. *'Agnes is still...*
that accident with the car...' Somewhere
there was a shift in the air's geographies
and Ellen stood behind the bar. Memories
came with her. I knew I had known her before.
There was a scuttering of claws on mesh.
I turned to see the monkey scraping the cage
in the window bay that overlooked the ridge.
'*Watch out for him,'* the woman said. *'Agnes*
hates him. He's always trying to bite.'
'*We got Rufus*,' Ellen said, *'after the parrot.*
Somebody opened the cage and let it out.
We searched the moor. Dead when we found it.'
Black dressed, she returned a polished glass
and her pose, her uplifted arm, broke memory,
drove recollection back into that day
of the hand-grenade's explosion, that chaos
of larks, that enduring echo of '*Dead.'*
I knew again that I had known her before.
I had seen soldiers quartering the moor,
their khaki ghosts a memory as they moved
now visible through the bay. Ellen grimaced.
'The ammunition dumps again.' 'At least
there's nobody hurt,' my fellow guest
seemed anxious to intrude and be included.
'I remember one being killed.' The limbo
of that old death consumed my mind,
and shuddered through me then. Ellen too, moved
in memory. *'That's a long time ago.*

I was courting then.' She twisted to review
her well-used plainness in the bar's mirror.
*'I can remember sliding to get down here,
to phone and call the ambulance.'* The screw
of Ellen's face was wry and unbelieving.
*'There was no telephone then. You couldn't -
not from here. Things might be different
if you had....'*

2.

'You couldn't have phoned from here.' There seemed
antagonism concealed in Ellen's
rebuttal of what I believed the prescience
of my memory. Not far away, outside,
without referral to the present, the fell
was bucking spring and I recalled the icon
stench of the moor, the lost larks in
fierce celebration, the nascent festival
of the year's businesses. Gaunt poles assaulted
the pub's white ride, bright water's psalters
ran whisky-gold over the millstone stairs
and that enduring, griping memory spawned
the exploding grenade. A lost time's urgency
called back my lungburst down through bracken
to batter at the pub's locked door and then
its slow and complex swing, its emery
scraping on rough stone. And she was there,
the girl in a black dress, her white arm raised.
I remembered the zebra of sunlight and shade
invading the room, while behind the bar,
brindling among the bottles and turning
liquor to tortoiseshell, light's flint exploded
in inverted gin. Ellen beside me said,
'You couldn't have phoned from here....'

3.

'You couldn't have phoned from here,' she said.
How could I be wrong? That day's incident
had lived and burned in me and no recant
was possible. That boy, long-shorted,
white spindle legs and bottle-bottom glasses,
that howling of *'Dead'* bursting to breach
the rim of the moor, that hurtle to reach
a telephone, nothing could ever erase.
'You couldn't have phoned from here.' There was
a yearning for some otherness in her voice,
something unreachable in her response,
a lost fulfilment. I could only guess.
Leaving, I passed the monkey's cage. *'Watch him,'*
the woman said. *'Agnes wants him gone*
she says he bites.' 'I've every reason
to remember,' Ellen insisted. *'At that time*
I was expecting a call. She couldn't ring.
*because there was no phone.' Outsi*de the door,
my own ghost waited, haunting the moor.
Black-haired, he waited. '*Dead'* he was shouting.

It seems a long time since we were dancing

1.

An old photograph. I remembered it
casually passed around, some reason
why it hardly mattered. Even by then
it was the faded relic of a night,
an end-of-season dinner, somewhere
expensive on the moor and I'd forgotten
its existence, until that later evening when
its twin appeared, enlarged, its register
of realities revealed and returned
untarnished from the album's open
neutrality. Madeleine was with me then
and she had often seemed concerned
that this was an image she believed had been
concealed deliberately from her.....
...and now, enlarged and so much glossier
more tellingly preserved, pristine
from the album's impartial imprisonment,
it emerged, a significant oracle,
to tell the treacheries and the betrayal
of that strange time, magnificently resonant
of our intrigues. In its intensification,
and through that still undamaged gloss,
its sharpness uncovered in each of us,
almost a Dorian Gray detection,
things hidden then, not solely from each other
but from ourselves, of which I'd had no sense
before: things that, on the lost evidence
of its diminished predecessor,
none of us would have known. In this
I came off badly and whatever
the multiplication of lost gesture
and past expression had been, so far as

Agnes then mattered, this new gloss
lit meanings in my eyes I might explain
to quell myself but would not have shown
before the others, or made so obvious
as to be plain even to Madeleine's
undoubted innocence. It might have led her
to question my previous reasons for
withholding, or hiding from her, what the lens
so patently displayed. This amplification
of its damaged twin's simplicity
might well have proved to her that we
were further apart than our convention
pretended or imagined. The glaze
of that magnesium flash had isolated
and advertised that my impaled
leering's direction was all for Agnes,
queen of that night's misrule, her mouth
recently emptied of her hints to me
of her flesh's willing availability.
There had been lewdness in her uncouth
offers and crude anticipations
of the uses I might have of her body,
suggestions whispered quietly
of how I might give her both gratification
and her revenge. My visible intent
was bursting for her, for me then, easily
the randiest and the most readily
available of the women present,
who, as we danced, salaciously
had offered me more than I knew how
to take from her flesh. I was callow
and a woman had never spoken to me
so openly, priming expectation
and suggesting the uses I might have
of her body. It lay beyond my naïve,
though tarnished innocence, that a woman

would ever use such curious coquetry
or make the proposals she had so calmly,
so tantalisingly and with such crudity.
tricked out in her flesh pledges to me.
By touch, by eye and by voice she promised
a readiness to move a dance more urgent.
The evidence of her availability lay latent
and licentious in my eyes and seemed
unmissable and unmistakable....

2.

'It seems a long time since we were dancing.'
She didn't say it but I knew by then
that that or some more recent version
would be the theme to sanitise our meeting.
It had, weighed and found wanting, seemed
a paltry and erratic thing between us.
Her urgent and erotic whispers
while we were dancing was now in need
of expiation more than explanation.
We needed a code, one that might mollify
her offering of herself, the crudity
of it all, her naked expression
of something that our years apart had caused me
to understand what she had needed.
And callow, I had failed to comprehend
the complex cause of her availability.
Later, I recognised that I had never been
the source of her excitement but her mere
actor for motives more arcane than pleasure,
to demonstrate a deeper concern.
What, at the time, I had been foolish enough
to gloat as passion for me had turned out,
to have its origins and its real root,
in the adultery she designed as proof,

of a direct and unequivocal avenge
to spite her husband's infidelities and never
more than a designed and insincere
disposal of her body and my leverage
towards her ends. Such substance as I
now gave it came from meanings reviewed
in a long retrospect. There was a charade
within an aura of never-again, a wry
pretence of continuing friendship,
bright smiles and certainly no bitterness
in an achievement marking her success
in matters more important than the flip
commodity of sex….and as I went
towards her, I remembered her appeal
as an attractive and almost beautiful
woman, certainly one whose intent,
in that unambiguous offering
while our dance continued, was hardly one
to be turned down, though on reflection,
it was a long time since we were dancing.

3.

'It seems a long time since we were dancing.'
Did she say it or have I invented it?
It was tangible in the room's conceit,
an ambiguity with a depending
intimation, a phrase that she knew would be
sufficient as camouflage and code.
And I remembered, as she intended,
a time before the accident when she
had the use of her legs and whispered
her acid recriminations, making it plain
that she was available. *'I was happy then,'*
she said. I wondered what alchemy had turned
that dross to gold. She had not been happy.

Agnes herself had probably been
at her most unhappy on an occasion
which seemed in a distorted memory
to have undergone a transformation
and transubstantiation. Such a material
adjustment of that night's betrayal
caused me to speculate how protean
things are. But it was a time for platitudes.
Whatever mood had been building,
and I remember its infiltration sliding
in snow outside and in the vicissitudes
of the plush room, that either one or both of us,
had opted to dissipate its danger.
Her prolonged imprisonment must have made her
alert to the expectations of others.
'I'm a lonely woman, Jack. But you can tell me
I was attractive once. Say I was worth a glance....
just to please me...that you fancied me once.'
She spoke self-mockingly to imply
her retreat. But there had been tears in her eyes
wearing the whiteness of reflected snow.
What she spoke was an ambiguous echo
of our long evanescent truths and lies.
Her glance fell to the splayed disarray
of paperback romances under her chair.
'I'm lonely, Jack. There's only Ellen here.
I could do with better company
than a big, coarse girl...'

4.

Ellen eyed me sourly. She carried a grenade
of the sort I'd seen often enough before,
some relic of the armaments of the moor.
It had been flattened and abraded
and through its centre a widened hole,

had held the coloured spills behind the bar.
'*I know you couldn't have phoned from here.'*
She set it down between us, her solid symbol
of our difference. *'And Agnes says she wants
to tell you something important.'* She spoke
facing the mirror, inventing some speck
on its surface. Between those incidents
I learned the source and substance of our quarrel
and saw my spoiling of the life she shared
with Agnes. I wondered how she'd heard
or guessed the knotted history of all
that nearly happened. The hand-grenade
stood now ironic for new distance,
and carried a more complex resonance
than I'd supposed. '*Not in here,'* she said.
'Never in here.' New ambiguities
veiled her warning. *'And I'd be hesitant.
Don't say too much. These days she doesn't want
reminders of your little secrecies...'*

5.

'What in hell ...' The lights were out. In those
first seconds it was bewildering.
'What bloody fool....what 's happening...'
I understood it clearly. The darkness was
my own, intentional and set to continue.
*'I know you couldn't have phoned from here.
She loved you once. Not now. You hurt her.*
Its mappings were of geographies I knew.
There was a sudden flaring and the dousing
of a match, a wavering point of redness
experiential in my blackout cosmos.
And then another match, its scraping
lighting in that uncertain matrix,
a candle, and in its early splutter,

the halo glow of a radiance no whiter
or wider than a face. As the wick's
osmosis fed the flame, the glow's expansion
lit different dimensions. And by then
I had expected it. I had long reason
to weigh its persisting accusation.
'You couldn't have phoned from here. You thought
she'd still be yours. Not now. No longer.'
It was then I saw the lank shock of hair,
the bottle-bottom glasses perching the white
moon of his face, his spindle legs and knew
our prolonged acquaintance. In one hand
the candle waved and smoked. The other held
a darkness supporting a pin-prick glow.
Certain that this could never be more
than trickery, my memory's travel
groped within seconds to that original
and witched hallucination of the moor,
Who else would know my landscapes? Only
the inside of a poem. Only one other.
You know you couldn't have phoned from here.
Couldn't you see she's mine? Can't you see why...'
At that time I was convinced the shapes
were no more than the candle's conjure,
apparitions shaped by the wax's gutter
in fickle air. They were my landscapes,
my inward history. My mind hunted
the secrets of their mirage manufacture.
Bottle-bottom glasses flashed, the flame's glimmer
moved on the moon of face and reached
the white, stalks of his legs. I guessed it
to be paltry and contrived, could see
the gist of what had been so cunningly
vouchsafed me as my golem boy twisted
and dissolved. The candle's trick presented
what I had known to expect. Within

the flame's guttering aureole, my demon
had laid his gift. I saw the serrated
grooving of latitude and longitude
shaping the segmentation that defined
the grenade's bulk. I watched its lighted,
pregnant intensity grow to invoke a crude
and feeble spluttering. In the rank reward
marking that spilling, he came ghastly
from the witched past, came towing to me
the fierce moralities of punctured
and penetrated flesh. *'Dead,'* he was shouting,
'You couldn't have phoned from here. You lied.
You lied to me. You lied to her. You tried...'
I recognised the sources of this witching.
The twitch of spark became a fountain,
a scintilla flame and in the lull
of its extinction, I waited to hear the spill
of the inevitable explosion.
Then it came. Not the reverberation
that once startled the crescent larks and
moved loaded through the moor's hinterland:
this time, only the squib detonation,
the flare of a penny firework. As I reached
towards it, warm from its petty swell
I questioned who could have known so well
the footpaths and the landscapes of my mind.
Only myself. The inside of a poem.
'You couldn't have phoned from here. You wish
she could still be yours. Your sort tarnishes...'
I held the metal docile in my palm,
traced its familiar serrations, knowing
the mercator projections of a different weight.
I knew it well. Ellen had carried its regret
through sunlight towards me, flaunting
its sour history. Time to recognise
that long since, I had elected waste,

had chosen the corrupted past,
my self-deceptions, my eroding lies.

6.
'...tarnishes.' Always I had moved
on maps of my own need. Each broken wall
and dead encampment had its footpaths plain,
was mythic to my route and fundamental
in all my journeys. On her I had drawn
marches of familiar landscape,
an arid terrain that I knew and when
its features were assembled, they would shape
a whole cartography of upland pain.

A tartan blanket

1.

'Come in, Jack.' Agnes's voice was clear.
The air's remembered tang that I'd encountered
with suspicion in the bar below had
followed me. On the table beside her,
her drink seemed the same as my own.
An ornate clock ticked loudly and slowly
and a tartan, some clan I couldn't identify,
covered her lower half. The collection
of paperback romances seemed the same
as I remembered. *'Is the fog still there?'*
She caused me to cross to the window where
heavily lined curtains filled the frame,
to draw them slightly and look out
to where the moor might be. The whole place
was insulated, immured now by a fog that was
eddying heavily and seemed to butt
urgently at the glass while turning
the room into a commodious limbo.
of old uncertainties. I stared into
that repudiating blankness, hearing
Agnes as she readjusted her position.

2.

When I turned to her, she sat more straightly,
the cast of her face and features strangely
altered and modified. The tartan
was lower around her waist. Lamplight
had failed to soften features which, though stress
had fixed them, were not malicious.
The subdued lighting of the room had brought
a beak-like hardening and deepening,

a hollowed, tightened quality to her face,
reshaping the contour of her eyes.
'It seems a long time since we were dancing.'
I had expected her words. The air was
pregnant with them. Once. there had seemed to be
a plangent, albeit hopeless quality
in the timbre of her tone and voice.
But this was very different, mocking
and ironic. Curtains that had failed
to fall completely together now revealed
the mist's corruption infiltrating
our mutual disloyalties before
the accident that took her legs away,
her cursing with a sour implacability
her husband's infidelities and sore
for revenge. Somewhere, time was astray.
'It seems a long time since we were dancing.'
I did not know if this were mere repeating,
or if her words had jumped in such a way
that I was hearing newer and unstated
meanings. There were entwined presences:
last time and this time in its occurrences:
moods past and present with a delayed
and ominous echo. It might well be that
neither was said. Lamplight's disorder
had dissolved her features' contour.

3.

I was no longer certain that the tartan blanket
was the one she had been wearing when
I entered, or was changed surreptitiously
while I looked towards the moor. Now, she
had moved back into another I had known
in our younger days. It lay lower
and looser on her, seemed that it might

fall from its covering duty. The white
blouse she wore, closed to her throat before,
had opened lower buttons. The light
from the lamp beside her, unequivocal,
touched now on the half-revealed swell
of her breast. What seemed a *jeune coquette*
had replaced her. I noticed only then
that the lipstick she wore was garishly
daubed to a redness almost certainly
years out of date, a gauche girl's fashion
and not a woman's make-up. Its smear
in the corner of her mouth made her seem
pathetic. '*Those years ago, that time,*
on that one night,' she said, *'I came so near*
to loving you... ' My memory's suggestion
held only the aura of her intent to sting
her husband, and myself the all-too-willing
mechanism. The clock had jerked on.

4.

The coquette, this lipsticked compromise
of past and present, of girl and woman
sat before me. Time had shuddered again.
'Could you make love to me tonight?' This
was the doll and never Agnes speaking.
I could not be sure that the puppet lips
before me had been moved except by slips
in some long and invisible string,
I looked at the unnatural creature
sitting before me, her shuddering outline
awaiting some re-shape and resolution
and knew then that the mordancy of the moor
had followed to torment me. Shadows danced
where there was no possibility
they might show movement *'Am I so ugly?*

Do I frighten you? I didn't frighten you once,
did I? You were greedy for me then.
I still have my needs. I'm playing the tart
and shaming myself, Jack, asking for that,
You wanted me then. I've not forgotten ...'

5.

I could not be certain of the unresolved
image before me. The puppet lips had moved
out of sequence with the words. I heard
the pendulum's slow swing. Time stuttered.
The clock's works had slipped, its ratchets
rattled another dimension. This shaped to be
another of those weird and visionary
moments on the fell. Another sun bounced its
old splendour on the moor's hinterland,
new bracken burgeoned the fell's awakening.
Like a screen shuddering in its searching
for programmed order, vibrating to find
its intended image, like something seen
through moving water, time readjusted
me Lazarus to revivify the dead.
'Tell me about Joe Anderson again.'
It came suddenly and without reason,
the innocent bathos of that day, that girl,
my once deceit in a sunshine unrepeatable.
And with her came that explosion
volleying through the moor with its enduring
reverberation. Black larks came with her
in territories more than familiar
and bleak. '*Dead,'* someone was shouting.

6.

Then the tartan blanket was the one that,
when I entered, had been folded close
about her waist and her white blouse
was chaste and fastened to her throat.
The curtains at the window were closed:
had never been opened. Paperback romances
were piled to decorate the valances
of her chair. It seemed we had moved
from the extremes of the imagined past
to the banalities of the present
and yet there remained some remnant
between us, lying inert but not yet lost
among the plush carpets, the stilled shadows,
the fake inn windows of the lampshades
beaming their icon of a simpler world's
domestic cheer. Something curious
had happened between us and she was
determined to ignore it. We had mouthed
its parts and in its necessities, performed
the gestures that something numinous
had demanded. I was now more certain
of the present we had distorted,
the writhing echoes of the past that had moved
between us. *'I've been a lonely woman.*
Sometimes I forget myself,' she said,
'and say more than I mean.' Her eyes fell
to the paperbacks. The clock's travel
ticked normality. Shadows insisted
that they had never moved, could not have moved.
'It seems a long time since we were dancing.'

Walking in Smoke

('Their witches sham death in delusion or delirium. This state, they call 'walking in smoke' and believe their souls fly from them to float the stars or rampage in some devil's satellite.')

1. Death of a Monkey

Rufus, outlandish, platyrrhine swung
in a cage spanning a window bay,
a gymnast enclosed, performing
against a moorland spawning a grey
light clawing ravenous at the glass.
Lulled by a thermostat, his supple limbs
played tropical against a foliage
of rushes and bare gritstone climbs.
Heretic heat one spidered night seduced
him to renegade. The moon's allure
garbled lost creeds of luxury and urged
escape to the cobwebbed continent of moor.
We found him mummified to gargoyle
within an overhang of shale and grit.
The famished inquisition of the fell
put to the question. Prehensile death
fixed the exotic leafage of his myth
in shrivelled contours. Spiders on the slope
membraned him, webbed him apostate,
stilled the dissent of an infertile hope.

2. Raptors

Fog thinly laminate on tarmac
broke at the car's buffet. The owl
dropped out of darkness in heraldic
headlong, a raptor's swoop to kill
its chrome reflection, a stuka strike

predatorial into the upthrust
belly of headlights. The famish beak
guided splayed talons through mist.
This was a death matadorial
in its short and ritual ferocity,
its conflict of flesh and metal.
Only one bled. Above, a clean sky
diminished the whole affair.
Cold planets skidded a moonless vault.
Stars arched imperial to concur
such happenings as the universe's fault
where predators collided in a friction
of competing energies. They were
mere accidents of light and misdirection
made treacherous by chrome's mirror.
Machineries of flesh and metal's innocence
had found their absolute in predatory
collision, the raptor's necessary lance,
the pistons' robotic anarchy.

3. Double Vision

The World's End stood once nameless,
modest, whitewashed within the acid
bright April sunshine, cloud shadow scudding
the reviving rumours of the moor,
scouring in knuckle outcrops, waking
the threadbare grasses. *The World's End* wore
my virgin landscapes, crowded the vault
bursting with larks. Gaunt poles ran,
quitting the road to file a thin assault
on the white walls. And then that burgeon
left me. Now, in a darkness, bitten by
the headlights' mince, that once region
paraded a gilded whore, wantonly
scraping allure's diminished invitation.

Gaudy illumination spilt the name:
bulbs spat their bauble into mist.
Someone shouted *'Rufus'*. At the time,
it meant nothing. Among the waste
of stars, one shuddering planet,
a clack of mindless laughter puncturing
the alien polish of the night.
I knew it then. *Something was going wrong.*

4. Cages

On the fell's flank, spirals of thin snow
balanced and spilled along the gullies.
That room shared with the bar below
Rufus's view. In her commodious
and like imprisonment, Agnes said,
'A long time since we danced.' She stirred,
leglessly reasserting what remained
of her once agile self. Open curtains bared
where the blanched barrenness of the fell,
echoed our past's emptiness. Easy to guess
that double frisson and our once double
treacheries, our cages' invalidities.
I remembered her whole and beautiful,
cursing her husband and implacable,
it seemed then, to compound and seal
a time when we had danced together. *'Tell
Hughie,'* she said, *'that Rufus frightens me.
I want that monkey gone. I know that he'll
listen to you.'* But she had grown
sensitive in her crippled sentence there,
guessing me loth to try with real conviction.
Again, my lies were bringing back to her
the cages of the past. *'I'll do my best.'*
Just as before, nothing would come of it.
It was a long time since we danced.

Tears touched her eyes reflecting white
snow trapped and whirling in gullies.
'I've been a lonely woman since –' Eyes were
dropped to the paperback romances
imprisoned, barren beneath my chair.

5. Walking in Smoke

Something was going wrong. Once in the bar,
I walked in smoke. My universe evolved
odours of past deceits, an older
moor's infidelities. And in that broomride,
an agaric otherness possessed me.
A night's mock Sabbat spawned the room,
gaudy and insincere on the witch upland,
wearing the fancy dress of beasts to assume
the prancing of animals. Nearer my mind,
irrational in its buzzing finery,
there came the bulging and prognathous
head of a bluebottle with plastic antennae
shivering my face to waken the mess
of Agnes's long boudoir captivity.
Glitter paint shaped the leaning orbit
of multiple eyes. Within that stare
was the malevolence and the implicit
enmity of the basilisk. Fingers were
strumming the mesh of Rufus's prison.
Somebody fiddled with the cage's lock,
'Give him his chance to join the fun -'
There was no fun. I walked in smoke
and heard again Agnes's pleading, saw
through the misted glass behind him,
our once deceit, a whirl of snow
twisting the landscapes of another frame.

Something was going wrong. Again
I walked in smoke. Again my cosmos
evolved the past's deceits, that coven
of broomride infidelities.
Again that agaric otherness
possessed me. My Beelzebub fly
had vanished. That Sabbat's gross
masquerading had left there only
some gaudy tokens of its existence.
The cage's lock was broken. I knelt
before its screech confessor. Rufus
heard *mea culpas* for promises unkept
and learned the carnal language
that Agnes and myself ingrained,
gibbering no absolution to assuage
atonement's need. Instead, he bit my hand.
It was his ambiguity to be held
both instrument and object of my promise.
A lost smock scarfing my hand, I hauled
doors from his stall and groped to squeeze
his space, to cassock him in the vesture
of that discarded cloth. Once more,
I walked in smoke, unfrocked him at the door,
to bundle his liberty into the moor.

6. Witches

Well, maybe Agnes. Disembodied litter
dressed the car park. A few animal
inventions and a mythic carnivore
grubbed among stones. My bluebottle
Beelzebub flapped antennae, octopus
on a stretched netting. Monstrosity
fluttered, wasting its once disguise
in bushes, its comic commodity
and plastic insincerity now useless,

already disintegrating. The world is
witchless enough and witches anyway,
were always fantasy. *And maybe Agnes.*
I saw the owl's body where it lay
and heard the land's language. Snow fell on
the inexplicable inscription
of stones: mist spoke the lost religion,
the old knowing. I felt the frisson
of a magic that queried reason's reaches
and groped to learn the planets' alchemies.
The world is witchless enough and witches
no more than fantasy. *Or maybe Agnes.*

Monkey business

1.

'Is that you, Jack?' The telephone's clatter
had jolted me from sleep. The night's mist
had burned to a thin sunlight. Naylor's interest
would be his own affairs. *'Some silly bugger
broke Rufus's cage and let him out. I could name
somebody bloody pleased to see him lost.'*
Agnes lay under his tongue. My first
concern had been for her, her part in the game
of their marriage. I dressed unwillingly.
My head ached. Driving into the fell,
pale sunshine fretted conditional
on the moor's reaches. Where the road runs awry,
swerving to avoid an insert coign,
there lay the feathered wreckage of an owl
and, poised for seconds, a wings-wide kestrel
hung in the wind's twisting distortion.

2.

In the car park's emptiness, Naylor waited
my driving there, a coffee steaming
between gloved hands. Last mist was clearing
from the fell's dome and swelling acid
in sunlight behind his shoulder. A thin
column of smoke was stringing his chimney
to brighter air above. *'I needed somebody...'*
His porch was strung with an unbroken chain
of webs, stray filaments glistening, billowing
in a freshening wind. At the car park's corner,
party streamers, snakes slithering the moor,
fluttered and writhed, striking at nothing,

from where, further down their coil,
wind failed to break a flimsy adherence
to drying asphalt. One spiralled sudden menace,
sidewinding into grass. *'Some bloody fool
cracked open his cage and forced the bloody lock...'*
Behind the building, the day's kestrel hung,
bracing to stoop there in a shuddering
stasis '*No help in that direction.'* Naylor's look
implied the undrawn curtains of Agnes's room.
Snakes moved with him, to breach the spiders'
entrapments. It was a day for predators.

3.

'I know it's useless searching, not much sense...'
I saw no likelihood though I followed him, coursing
from right to left of him and slowly searching,
with not much diligence and little credence,
among the skirt and trailing concealment
of the gullies. Naylor was over the crest
and out of sight, his detective zest
leading him into the moor. My own hunt
took in the marshes behind the building.
I knew it useless, no more than a gesture
within the game between us. Foul water
and broken rushes modelled what long hung
latent between us. Brackish rivulets ran
through a compacted shale. A fickle
sunshine flickered in marches over the pale
mesh of the moor. It must have been then
I saw the kestrel's hovering question,
riding intently in some slow compass
of stiller air, poising in a hiatus
of recognition and a sharp rejection.
Expecting nothing, I scrambled to reach
and rout within the fringing edges of shale.

Naylor was waving semaphore, some signal
conveying the hopelessness of our search.
My eyes re-shaped the camouflage beneath
the kestrel's interest. Rufus lay knotted
and shrivelled there. Spiders had shrouded
his foetus folding. More than a monkey's death
was with me. The past's deceits and tensions
inhabited the closing space between us,
a latent and electrical unease,
an intensity of unspoken questions.

4.

I left Rufus to lie but signalled Naylor
urgently towards me. He came quickly,
loose shale slipping under him in the gully,
dropping his pace, unbalanced and unsure,
his footing slipping before he stooped and reached
through sodden fronds to loosen the creature,
scraping the webs from congealing fur
and totally unaffected. '*Stupid sod.*'
Once on the moor, I wondered what he saw
or won from that shrivelled homunculus.
Then suddenly, unprovoked, impetuous,
and in an elastic energy, he threw
the body high in the air. I thought,
at first. that he was shaping to volley it
in its descent towards us, but still acute
in his reflexes, at the last moment,
he stayed his movement to catch it in its fall
an inch from the ground. Again in his hand,
the body held its foetal form, unloosened
since the gully. Once over the ridge, the road
came into sight, the white pub handsome
in an evanescent sunlight under the dome.
In Agnes's window, the curtain fluttered.

He turned, sardonic towards me. *'I could name*
somebody really happy at what you've found.'
Something waited. Its mood had kestrelled,
growing between us in that morning's game.

5.

'I'll tell you this, Jack –' the moor's resonances
were gathering about me as he dangled
the monkey's corpse from an extended hand
towards the building. *'She's going to bless*
your handiwork. She's never fancied Rufus.
But she fancied you.' Till then, I'd never known
how much he knew. For years, the question
unasked, unanswered had hovered between us.
The buried malignancies and deceits
of the moor were with me then: that golem boy,
his crescent larks fomenting my dishonesty:
that pregnant girl: the null adulteries
of Agnes's intention: all the clumsy freight
of the past. *'And then that bloody accident...'*
I knew his guilt, remembered the bloody event,
her broken body after the drunken night.
Bushes still fluttered the spiders' industry.
The snakes had ribboned into the moor.
Ellen stood waiting, aloof, not far from the door.
'Jack found him.' He waved the congealed monkey
coarsely towards her. She said nothing.
'In the marshes.' he said. *'Beyond the pasture.*
This side of the quarries.' She made no gesture
of sympathy, though I knew that something
both strong and tacit had passed between them.
She signalled Agnes's still open window
and tried to take the monkey from him. *'No,'*
she shouted. *'No. Not that.'* It was a scream
and never the voice or tone of a hireling...

6.

He held the monkey from her, spiders' thread
trailing its bundle as they played out
a disagreement between equals and one not
between a hireling and employer. She had
understood his purposes and intended
to frustrate them, had heard but ignored
my interruption, still meaning to impede
his movement past her through the webs' blockade.
'No, Hughie. No. Not that.' She grappled
to take the monkey and stood her ground to hinder
his passage but he shielded Rufus from her.
She had no answer to the feint he made,
lunging wrongly and clumsily for him
while he moved past her other side. *'Just stay.*
Don't follow him,' she ordered me sharply,
turning to chase him. There was a scream.
'She won't want you up there till this is over.'
Agnes wailed from above and Ellen,
a new and raw concern marking her then,
almost the gesture and expression of a lover,
had started her lumbering chase on the stairs ….

bare + lea: Old English bær (bare, exposed) + lēah (woodland clearing, meadow) yields bare-lea meaning "exposed clearing" or "infertile/open ground." Phonetically this can produce forms like bareley / barley in later spelling, so a name recorded as "Barley" might derive from "bare lea" rather than the grain.

www.ingramcontent.com/pod-product-compliance
Lightning Source LLC
LaVergne TN
LVHW010101110826
845155LV00028B/441